THE
RORSCHACH
GOD

Copyright © 2024 by Matthew Hester

Published by Unorthodox Resources

All rights reserved. No portion of this book may be reproduced, stored in a retrieval system, or transmitted in any form or by any means—electronic, mechanical, photocopy, recording, scanning, or other—except for brief quotations in critical reviews or articles, without prior written permission of the author.

Unless otherwise specified, all Scripture quotations are taken from The ESV® Bible (The Holy Bible, English Standard Version®), copyright © 2001 by Crossway, a publishing ministry of Good News Publishers. Used by permission. All rights reserved. | Scripture quotations marked KJV are taken from the King James Version of the Bible. Public domain. | Scripture quotations marked MSG are taken from THE MESSAGE, copyright © 1993, 1994, 1995, 1996, 2000, 2001, 2002 by Eugene H. Peterson. Used by permission of NavPress. All rights reserved. Represented by Tyndale House Publishers, Inc. | Scripture quotations marked NASB are taken from the (NASB®) New American Standard Bible®, Copyright © 1960, 1971, 1977, 1995, 2020 by The Lockman Foundation. Used by permission. All rights reserved. www.lockman.org | Scripture quotations marked NIV are taken from the Holy Bible, New International Version®, NIV®. Copyright © 1973, 1978, 1984, 2011 by Biblica, Inc.™ Used by permission of Zondervan. All rights reserved worldwide. www.zondervan.com. The "NIV" and "New International Version" are trademarks registered in the United States Patent and Trademark Office by Biblica, Inc.™ | Scripture quotations marked NKJV are taken from the New King James Version®. Copyright © 1982 by Thomas Nelson. Used by permission. All rights reserved.

For foreign and subsidiary rights, contact the author.

Cover design by Sara Young
Cover photo by Andrew van Tilborgh

ISBN: 978-1-962401-75-3   2 3 4 5 6 7 8 9 10

Printed in the United States of America

WHAT PEOPLE ARE SAYING ABOUT *THE RORSCHACH GOD*

For centuries, scholars and seekers of God have studied Scripture to answer the big question, "Who is God and what is He like?" After two thousand years, what more can be said? As it turns out, a lot! With Matthew Hester's release of *The Rorschach God*, we are given a fresh template to study these age-old questions. In my reading of previous attempts, I found a flaw, one that Hester skillfully avoids and guides us in a new direction. The flaw lies in giving all of Scripture equal authority in determining the nature of God. Yes, Jesus was part of those studies, and therein lies the problem. Attempting to fit Jesus into centuries of a partial and incomplete view of God simply does not work. Hester, however, looks at Jesus first and foremost as the perfect reflection of God. It is time to move beyond a flat interpretation of Scripture and let the words of the new creation be the final authority, as it is written, "He (Jesus) is the radiance of the glory of God and the exact imprint of his nature" (Hebrews 1:3, ESV). Why look anywhere else? There are plenty of books to read, too many perhaps, yet this one should be at the top of your list as it offers a fresh perspective on who we worship, who we serve, and the God we proclaim to the world.

—Dr. Stan Newton
Author, President of Crown Institute of Theology

The famous quote goes, "We don't see things as they are, we see them as WE are." As a result, we (the human race) have, throughout history, projected images of ourselves upon God, thus misrepresenting Him to the world around us. And as a result of doing so, we've often done more damage than good both to ourselves as well as to others. In *The Rorschach God*, Matthew Hester will take you on a powerful journey that will illuminate your mind to start seeing the truth that has always been there from the beginning. The pages throughout this thought-provoking book will cause your human conditioning to be removed from the equation so you can start to see things for what they truly are. By the time you're finished reading, you'll have given up the desire to try to create a "god" in your image. Instead, you'll re-awaken to the truth of your being that you are, and have always been, created in His image. I encourage everyone to allow *The Rorschach God* to "turn the lights on" so that you can become a witness of the true nature of God as well as the abundant life that He has in store for us all.

—Martijn van Tilborgh
Author, Speaker, Entrepreneur, Co-Founder of AVAIL

In *The Rorschach God*, Dr. Matthew Hester offers a unique and thought-provoking perspective on the age-old question: "Who is God?" Hester compellingly reveals how our understanding of God's character is often shaped by our own projections and biases, much like ambiguous inkblots unveil the viewer's inner world. With theological depth and pastoral sensitivity, Hester guides us from the shadows of fallen mindsets, religious misconceptions, and cultural biases to embrace the true likeness of God revealed in Christ. This book is a must-read for anyone ready to challenge their assumptions and discover a God who is far more loving, gracious, and relational than they have been taught or imagined.

—Schlyce Jimenez
Author, Founder of Emerge School of Transformation

Dr. Matthew Hester believes God is good. And I would venture to say that he perhaps believes that God is better than even you, the reader, think He is. Thought leaders like Dr. Hester are both threatening and revolutionary in light of modern religious thinking. And yet, they are necessary and needed to cause us to reconsider any notions that we may have about God that have not been subjected to honest scrutiny. I am not challenged at all by those who deem God as a necessary choice, and also as an occasionally abusive monster. But I am wonderfully challenged by those who refuse to ascribe any other identity to Him than as an unconditionally loving, infinitely merciful, and unfailingly trustworthy Father. Dr. Hester is the latter, and in reference to God's overall character and nature, he takes his cues from Jesus Christ. This book will disempower the grip that fear has had on your perspective of God and open your heart to a communion of intimacy with a loving Father. I can confidently say that *The Rorschach God* will challenge your divine perspective deeply, and I encourage you to take the journey.

—Bill Vanderbush
Author, Speaker

It's about time a book has come out that challenges the way you view God, the Bible, and Jesus. Let's be honest, the current way is not working. It's not bearing any fruit.

I've had the privilege of reading through *The Rorschach God* by Dr. Matthew Hester, a book that I firmly believe is indispensable for anyone seeking to grasp the proper hermeneutical approach to the Scriptures. This work challenges conventional perspectives and invites readers into a deeper, more authentic engagement with the Word of God.

Dr. Hester challenges us to see beyond traditional interpretations and to view God through the lens of Jesus Christ's life and teachings. One of the most powerful aspects of the book is how it encourages us to question our old perceptions and biases about God. The discussions on the Beatitudes and the Sermon on the Mount invite us into a transformative understanding of these passages, showing us that Jesus's teachings are about active, radical love—not just rules to follow.

My friendship with Matthew and his wife, Megan, has shown me their deep commitment to truth and clarity in understanding Scripture. Dr. Hester's passion is palpable on every page of this book, making complex theological concepts accessible and engaging.

The Rorschach God is essential for those who are ready to challenge their views and embrace a more authentic, heartfelt approach to God. It's not just about reading another book on theology—it's about changing how we live out our faith every day. This book is a call to refocus—a call to stop doing things our way, or even the ways of the sinful men and women mentioned in Scripture. It's a call to be Christian, to be more like Christ every day.

—Johnny Ova
Pastor and former Pro Wrestler

Jesus is perfect theology. I first heard that statement almost 20 years ago and have been unpacking it in transformative ways ever since. I agree with Matthew—it's both "simple and profound."

Matthew is a friend and a forerunner in the goodness of God. In this beautiful book, he "encourages us to ask deeper, more meaningful questions that challenge our existing perceptions and assumptions."

What we believe about the nature of God determines everything—what we believe about ourselves, one another, and how we navigate faith and life. *The Rorschach God* is a brilliant invitation to rethink; to discover and invite Jesus into our bias, illusions, broken experiences, disappointments, and our Western theological assumption of separation.

For too long we, the church, have fashioned God in the likeness of our pain, shame, or some preacher's fear. But Jesus is what God has to say about Himself and He revealed that God is not angry at, disappointed of, or ashamed of us. He isn't wagging His finger or condemning. He hasn't left or forsaken us, and never will. In fact, before the foundations of the world, God was in Christ reconciling us to Himself, loving, forgiving, restoring, and transforming us! And this book is an invitation to discover and know this stunning God!

Matthew has spent his life studying, ministering, and practicing love. He writes with humility and compassion. He writes with theological integrity while never communicating over our heads. I believe there is liberty, joy, and peace available in the pages of this book!

—Jason Clark
Author of *Leaving and Finding Jesus*, Host of
Rethinking God with Tacos PODCAST

Dr. Matthew Hester creatively challenges the often-held view of a distant and wrathful God. With engaging language and modern examples, he illustrates how Jesus truly embodies God's essence—loving, forgiving, and deeply relational. *The Rorschach God* invites readers to reconsider their perspectives, presenting a more compassionate and accurate depiction of God as demonstrated by Jesus, and encourages a deeper, kinder understanding of the divine.

—Channock Banet
Pastor, Co-host of *Two Pastors and a Mic* PODCAST

Dr. Matthew Hester uses brilliant and clever language to portray the God who looks like Jesus: a God who desires relationship and is characterized by beauty and love. He invites you to dance with this God. Hester unpacks theology in a way that will provoke your imagination to remove the "Rorschach" imagery of a violent and vengeful God and embrace the non-violent and restorative God revealed in the person of Jesus—the true image of God.

—Dr. Cory Rice
Author, Cohost of *Two Pastors and a Mic* PODCAST

My friend Matthew Hester has done a masterful job in his new book *The Rorschach God*. It is a must-read for leaders and those who wrestle with difficult portions of scripture, as well as for those who take the Bible seriously enough to question it. I want to encourage everyone to get a copy and at least consider that our Western, flat reading of scripture is inadequate and that we have to do better for the sake of our children and grandchildren. We are seeing tens of thousands of our young people walk away from the faith because a college professor destroys their understanding of the Bible in one philosophy class by presenting terrifying verses that were never explained to them, as well as things that seem contradictory.

On the Emmaus road, Jesus opened up the scriptures to the two disciples whose hearts were burning within them, or we could say that Jesus interpreted the Old Testament and not the other way around. A Christocentric hermeneutic is what Jesus and the apostles revealed to us by how they interpreted the Old Testament. We do not just read the Bible, but the Bible also reads us, and it reflects who we think God is and who we really are.

When I was an angry preacher, I focused on the angry, wrathful God verses. But when I was transformed by an encounter with His love, I began to see His love for me and the world on every page. Scripture can be a mirror that reflects who we are, just as it also shows us who God is.

—Jamie Englehart
Author, Overseer of C.I.M. Network

It has been said that we become like the God that we believe in. Or in the words of Voltaire, "In the beginning God created man in His own image, and man has been trying to repay the favor ever since." In *The Rorschach God*, Matthew Hester has addressed the many caricatures, or ludicrously exaggerated and misguided memes, of God's truest essence. You will find in each chapter the lens of your understanding being adjusted to gain a clear and crisp perception of a good, gracious, and loving God. Expect to experience a few epiphanies where you will find yourself saying, "Who are You? And where have You been all my life?"

—Dr. Randall Worley
Author of *Brush Strokes of Grace* and *Wandering and Wondering*

The Rorschach God is a fresh, vulnerable, and rich exploration of how humanity, as seen in scripture and experience, tends to create God in its own image. Jumping off of his personal struggle and professional quandary as a teacher and pastor with a God of Love, Who in so many cases seems opposite, Matthew masterfully dives into scripture, hermeneutics, and how church fathers were able to bridge contradiction and paradox. Seeing God in the face of Jesus Christ as a starting point allows us to begin to see the scary angry God of separation and condemning judgment as the antithesis of Who God truly is. What has been antithetical to God as seen through the lens of Christ is truly anti-Christ.

When wrestled with honesty and rigorousness, what remains with all the trouble scripture and doctrines of men is the God, Who we desperately need and intuitively long for. This is a God Who is for and not against us; a God Who sacrifices on behalf of us as His beloved kids and doesn't impose sacrifice to earn anything. This God adores us when we are at our worst and dives into our worst to fish us out of our own delusions and destructiveness for our sakes. Here is a God of relentless pursuit of everything lost in us and all creation. This God transfigures us as His kids, not because He finds us repulsive in our fallen ways of being, but because we are too holy, lovely, powerful, and precious to be less than we truly are.

Matthew has taken pains to wrestle with what church fathers grappled with as well as re-approaching scripture so that it can be restored as the life-giving gift that it was intended without doing violence to it by ignoring what is there. He has done the work himself so that what comes out is refreshing and genuine, not preachy or a rehash. Thank you, Matthew, for this work which will help so many with the tricky, "God-is-Love-but-what-about?" questions that plague us. I wholeheartedly endorse Matthew's book and look forward to what will undoubtedly follow!

—Catherine Toon, MD
Author, Speaker, Coach,
Founder & CEO of Imprint & Catherine Toon Ministries

The book you're about to read is more than a book. It is a compass guiding us toward TRUE NORTH. For years I sought after a book that reveals the very things that *The Rorschach God* makes so plain to us. This book struck me so deeply that I immediately thought "I need a version for my kids (yep, my kids)."

Written within the pages are keys that only those carried by The Wind receive. There is a massive gap today in Western culture with how we view God and the way Jesus actually revealed Him to be. *The Rorschach God* bridges that gap and provides a safe and secure bridge between the God of our own making and the one Jesus revealed to us.

Matthew has a unique ability to share these truths in such a way that every son and daughter can, by "help of Holy Spirit," receive them. He writes with theological integrity and scholarly precision, and most of all, with the heart of a son that longs to see and reveal Papa to us. I pray that this writing will do for you what it has begun to do in me. Thank you, Matthew Hester!

—Joshua Jones
Pastor

I really enjoyed reading this book. It is both challenging and stimulating. Reading this book made me rethink some ideas that I had believed in for a long time, like the two disciples who walked with Jesus on the Emmaus Road after the resurrection, I am once again reminded that Jesus is perfect theology. I was motivated to think through a paradigm that was different from mine yet fresh and alive. Matthew is a fresh voice of the relational revolution. His words in this book are calling us to live like Jesus. I hope others will read the book and come away with a renewed vision of Jesus and be better for it. Matthew lives what he teaches in this book, and that fresh touch of love is so needed in our world. In reading this book, you may, like the disciples, come away with the same thought, "Were not our hearts burning within us?" Great job! As you read it, be prepared to be amazed.

—Roy Rhodes, Pastor, Founder of Treasures of Joy Ministries

The great George MacDonald famously wrote the words, "Good souls many will one day be horrified at the things they now believe of God." I like to think that works like Matthew Hester's *The Rorschach God* will help such "good souls" have far fewer things to be horrified at on the day they behold God as He truly is. I am convinced that we are in the middle of what will go down in history as having been something like a new Great Awakening, and Hester's words, offered in this amazing work, only add volume to the loving, gentle, but passionate alarm bell that is presently ringing throughout the world, piercing the shrill, cacophony of lies MacDonald tells us we will one day be horrified at having ever fallen for. In *The Rorschach God*, Hester calls a generation of disillusioned daughters and sons out of the illusions and delusions of a fear-based faith to—instead—behold the face of a God in whom there has never been anything to fear.

—Jeff Turner
Author of *Saints in the Arms of a Happy God* and *The Atheistic Theist*

...you thought I was exactly like you...

THE
RORSCHACH
GOD

DR. MATTHEW HESTER

This book is dedicated to everyone who is searching out the character and nature of God as is revealed through the Person of Jesus. We refuse to worship a god of our own making.

CONTENTS

Introduction 17

CHAPTER 1. Shadows of the Divine 23

CHAPTER 2. God Stayed Silent 33

CHAPTER 3. The Role of Scripture 51

CHAPTER 4. Whatever Happened to the Trinity? 69

CHAPTER 5. The Sermon on the Mount:
 The Jesus (Godhead) Way 87

CHAPTER 6. What About the Violent God? 109

CHAPTER 7. What About the God Who
 Craves Sacrifice? 127

CHAPTER 8. What Is God's Ideal? 139

CHAPTER 9. The Enemy's Table 153

CHAPTER 10. The Father Is Life, Light, and Love 165

EPILOGUE The Road to Emmaus 183

The Rorschach test is a projective psychological test in which subjects' perceptions of inkblots are recorded and then analyzed using psychological interpretation, complex algorithms, or both. Some psychologists use this test to examine a person's personality characteristics and emotional functioning.

Recommended Resources from Present Truth Academy:
- *Trinity*
- *The God Who Looks Like Jesus*
- *Union With Christ*
- www.PresentTruthAcademy.org/shop

INTRODUCTION

Have you ever found yourself strolling through the journey of life, confidently holding onto your beliefs and convictions, only to encounter a piece of information that challenges everything you thought to be true? It's like the ground shifting beneath your feet, compelling you to reconsider your long-standing perspectives. While such experiences can certainly be intimidating, they can also serve as catalysts for substantial growth. The key to navigating such moments is to be unafraid to explore powerful questions and allow for the presence of mystery.

As I'm presented with new ideas, I find myself reflecting on the power of storytelling to challenge perceptions and upend expectations. It's like revisiting cherished movies that masterfully execute this feat, leaving us astounded in a single viewing. Take, for instance, the iconic transformation of Darth Vader in *Return of the Jedi*. Throughout the saga, he epitomizes the ultimate antagonist, only to undergo a profound change of heart when confronted with the suffering of his own son, Luke Skywalker. Suddenly, he becomes the unexpected hero, defying the tyrannical Emperor Palpatine to save his son and redeem himself.[1]

Similarly, the journey of Gru in the *Despicable Me* franchise serves as another compelling example. Initially portrayed as a

---
1 Richard Marquand, *Return of the Jedi* (May 25, 1983; Los Angeles, CA: 20th Century Studios).

diabolical supervillain, Gru's encounter with a trio of orphaned girls sparks a profound transformation within him. Their influence softens his heart, leading him to embrace his role as a nurturing father figure and ultimately evolve into a hero.[2]

And who could forget Harrison Ford's character in *What Lies Beneath*? Known predominantly for his heroic roles, Ford's portrayal in this suspenseful thriller takes a riveting turn as he unveils a darker, more sinister side. The revelation of his character's true nature adds layers of complexity to the narrative, keeping audiences on the edge of their seats and underscoring the power of unexpected storytelling twists.[3]

Several years ago, I underwent a major "plot twist" within the world of my personal faith—a journey that overturned my longstanding beliefs and challenged much of my imaging concerning the character and nature of God. For some perspective, I've been deeply involved in various facets of ministry for the majority of my life. For more than twenty years, I've ministered around the world, spreading the gospel and serving as a pastor alongside my wife since 2015. Along the way, I've pursued higher education, earned a doctorate in theology, and founded the Present Truth Academy—an online school dedicated to sharing what I believed to be the forefront of cutting-edge truth within the body of Christ. I share these experiences not to boast, but to underscore the depth of my involvement and unwavering commitment to the Christian faith.

Amidst my many endeavors, I often found myself expending significant energy defending depictions of God that appeared

---

[2] Chris Renaud and Pierre Coffin, *Despicable Me* (July 9, 2010; Los Angeles, CA: Universal Pictures).
[3] Robert Zemeckis, *What Lies Beneath* (July 21, 2000; Glendale, CA: DreamWorks Pictures).

to contradict the loving and compassionate Father I intimately knew. Despite my deep-rooted belief in a patient and merciful God, I encountered passages in Scripture that portrayed a deity seemingly devoid of such qualities. For instance, verses like Jeremiah 13:14 depict God as unyielding, vowing not to let mercy or compassion prevent the destruction of families. Similarly, passages such as 1 Samuel 15:2-3 recount commands for the Israelite army to mercilessly annihilate entire populations, including men, women, children, and even animals. These instances, among many others, presented a disturbing dichotomy that challenged my understanding of divine character. How could I reconcile these narratives of sacrifice, violence, natural disasters, disease, slavery, polygamy, and more with my perception of a benevolent and compassionate God?

Wrestling with such discrepancies became a nearly exhausting struggle, leading me to question how I could continue to defend such portrayals of God. I wouldn't go so far as to say that these images stopped me from trusting God or caused me to begin questioning His existence, but I reached a point where I grew weary of witnessing the continual misrepresentations of God's true nature. Seeking clarity and some kind of peace for my spirit, I delved into various theological frameworks, exploring systems such as Reformed theology, Charismatic theology, the New Apostolic Reformation, Covenant Theology, and beyond. While each offered richness and compelling arguments, I found myself encountering deficiencies within each perspective that left me unsatisfied. Despite the insights gained from these studies, none fully aligned with what I deeply knew about the One who is abundant in mercy, and driven by the immense love He has for us (see Ephesians 2:4).

After years of studying, ministering, and practicing God's love, the ultimate revelation finally came: Jesus. Reflecting on the Bible from Genesis to Jesus's arrival, a stark contrast emerged between the various depictions of God and His true essence. The Old Testament presented conflicting images of God, but Jesus unraveled the mystery. As the exact image of the Father, Jesus revealed God's love, grace, compassion, and righteousness. He bridged the gap between humanity and divinity, reshaping my understanding of God.

Rediscovering the ancient doctrines and esteemed figures of the faith filled me with immense joy. I embarked on a journey of fresh exploration into both Trinitarian Theology and a more robust Christology. I began digging into the profound insights of the Finished Work perspective and immersed myself in Kingdom Theology. Alongside these theological inquiries, I expanded my reading horizons far beyond the scope of my traditional Protestant framework. Venturing into the rich wisdom of Eastern traditions of faith, I discovered invaluable insights that enhanced my spiritual understanding. At first, I thought my faith would become very narrow, but instead, it was broadened to help me recognize and more deeply embrace the vast tapestry of Christian thought, belief, and tradition.

Discovering the writings of the Patristic fathers like Athanasius, Gregory of Nazianzus, and John Chrysostom brought me great joy. I embraced the insights of revered voices within the Catholic tradition, finding immense value in works such as Father Richard Rohr's transformative book *The Divine Dance*, which remains among my top five favorites of all time. I also drew wisdom from contemporary scholars like Greg Boyd, whose writings deeply influenced the thoughts reflected in this book. Additionally, voices such as George MacDonald, Thomas F. Torrance, Brian Zahnd, Brad Jersak, John Crowder, William Paul Young, and C. Baxter Kruger, whom I regard as a personal hero, offered invaluable wisdom that developed my understanding of a more Christlike faith. These voices, along with many others, have cultivated a desire for the gospel of my life to be a harmonious blend of treasures both old and new, all converging to communicate the beautiful simplicity of the gospel.

This book doesn't attempt to construct a brand-new theological framework or provide definitive answers to every theological question. Instead, its purpose is to encourage us to ask deeper, more meaningful questions that challenge our existing perceptions and assumptions. I pray it catalyzes introspection and urges you to set aside distorted images of God that your own desires, needs, and limitations have shaped. Simply stated, Jesus won't allow our "Rorschach Imagery" of the Father to remain intact. Rather than offering conclusive solutions, the aim is to focus on the person of Jesus Christ to facilitate a clearer understanding of the divine. I pray this book, in some small way, illuminates the character of God as revealed through Jesus and thus enhances your perception and deepens your relationship with our always-good Father.

It's prudent here in the introduction that I acknowledge that no book, including this one, can fully encapsulate the depth of revelation that God desires to impart to you. God is pleased that we know things about Him, and He's fine with us sharing what we discover to help others on their faith journeys. But He never wants us to substitute our knowledge of Him for engaging with Him intimately. I get it, intimacy is risky and we all crave a sense of control in our relationships, but God invites us into vulnerability and authentic connection. It's in this space of openness and intimacy that we truly encounter and experience the depth of His love and presence in our lives. As you journey onward, may this book serve as a guide, but may your deepest encounters with God come through the profound intimacy of your personal relationship with Him and, by extension, with your neighbor.

> "God mediates his revelation to human beings in such a way that he accommodates his self-revealing to human knowing and adapts human knowing to receive and apprehend what he reveals in ways that are appropriate to it."—Thomas F. Torrance, *The Mediation of Christ* [4]

> "God loves us more than a father, mother, friend, or any else could love, and even more than we are able to love ourselves."—Saint John Chrysostom[5]

---

4 Thomas Forsyth Torrance, *The Mediation of Christ* (Colorado Springs, CO: Helmers & Howard Publishers, July 1, 1992).
5 "John Chrysostom (347-407) Archives," *Catholic Storeroom*, www.catholicstoreroom.com/category/quotes/quote-author/john-chrysostom-347-407/page/6/.

CHAPTER 1

SHADOWS OF THE DIVINE

In a small, dimly lit office, Emily sat nervously awaiting her turn to take the Rorschach test. She fidgeted with her hands, her mind racing with apprehension. Dr. Patel, a kind-eyed psychologist, prepared the inkblot cards with methodical precision.

"Emily, we're ready to begin," Dr. Patel said, his voice gentle yet probing. "I'll show you a series of inkblots, and I want you to tell me what you see. There are no right or wrong answers, only your honest perceptions."

Emily nodded, her heart fluttering with uncertainty as she braced herself for the first inkblot. It appeared before her, a shapeless blot of ink sprawled across the white card.

"What do you see, Emily?" Dr. Patel inquired, his gaze fixed on her.

Emily studied the inkblot, her brow furrowing in concentration. "I see . . . darkness," she whispered, her voice trembling slightly. "Like a void swallowing everything in its path."

Dr. Patel nodded, jotting down notes on his pad. He moved on to the next card, and then the next, each one presenting Emily with a new puzzle to decipher.

With each inkblot, Emily's unease grew. She saw images of abandonment, of betrayal, of a presence looming ominously over her. It was as if the inkblots reflected her deepest fears and doubts, casting shadows over her fragile psyche. As the test progressed, Emily felt herself sinking deeper into despair. The inkblots seemed to mock her, their elusive forms twisting and contorting into grotesque shapes. She felt as though an unseen force, its presence looming heavy in the air, was judging her.

But amidst the darkness, a flicker of hope emerged. With each inkblot, Emily began to question her perception of the divine. She saw images of suffering, of injustice, of a god who remained silent in the face of human anguish. Finally, after what felt like an eternity, they reached the last card. Emily's hands trembled as she gazed at the final inkblot, its form swirling with ambiguity.

"And what do you see here, Emily?" Dr. Patel asked, his voice cutting through the oppressive silence.

Emily stared at the inkblot, her mind reeling with conflicting emotions. And then, with sudden clarity, she saw it. "I see . . . a fractured image," she whispered, her voice tinged with sadness. "A god who is both loving and indifferent, who watches over us yet remains distant."

A sense of disillusionment washed over Emily as she uttered those words, as if she had peeled back the veil of her faith to reveal the harsh truth beneath. The inkblots had been a mirror, reflecting the complexities of her relationship with the divine, but they had also been a catalyst for self-discovery.

When Emily left Dr. Patel's office that day, she couldn't shake the feeling of emptiness that lingered within her. The Rorschach test had shattered her illusions of a benevolent god, leaving her feeling adrift in a world devoid of meaning. As she stepped out into the cold embrace of the night, she wondered if she would ever find solace in the shadows of the divine.

Colossians 2:17 says, "These are a shadow of the things to come, but the substance belongs to Christ."

> *"God created man in His image, And man, being a gentleman, returned the favor."* —Author Unknown

Much of the world sees God in the same way Emily does. He comes across as both benevolent and indifferent, as unconditionally loving and eternally condemning, as forgiving but grudge-holding. God is more likened to a demigod of Greek mythology than one who is altogether lovely and holy. What's even worse is that Scripture often appears to support the bad imagery! How can we reclaim the image of God? How can we clearly and authentically see His heart and nature? I think I know a good place to start.

WHAT PEOPLE EXPECT TO SEE AND HEAR STRONGLY CONDITIONS WHAT THEY SEE AND HEAR.

The issue we face as believers is how to acquire the most accurate representation of God as we possibly can. To have this accurate imaging, we have to go to the source of God's nature most perfectly displayed. We must find the perfect reflection of God in Jesus. Jesus is perfect theology. This statement is loaded; it's both simple and profound. It is futile to try to understand God in a healthy way outside of the Person of Jesus.

What people expect to see and hear strongly conditions what they see and hear. Along the same lines, people can only receive the truth about God to the degree that their innermost hearts are aligned with His character. The good news is that John proclaims that when Christ appears, "we shall be like him, for we shall see him as he is," which is why "all who have this hope in him purify themselves, just as he is pure" (1 John 3:2-3, NIV). While all who are in Christ have had the veil over their minds "taken away" and can therefore "contemplate the Lord's glory" (2 Corinthians 3:14, 18, NIV), we still "see only a reflection as in a mirror" (1 Corinthians 13:12, NIV). But when the process of our transformation into Christlikeness is completed, we will finally have the capacity to grasp Christ in all His beauty. And it is only because "we shall be like him," that we will finally be able to "see him as he is."

Jesus taught that all Scripture is about Him and that He is the life of Scripture (see John 5:39-40). Curiously enough, Jesus immediately went on to tell the Pharisees that they were incapable of accepting this truth, even though they studied Scripture diligently. And the reason, Jesus said, is because they did "not have the love of God in [their] hearts" (John 5:42, author paraphrase).

Clearly, discerning how all Scripture points to Jesus requires more than diligent study. Jesus is the perfect revelation of God's love, and only those who have a heart to embrace and trust this love can discern how it is reflected in all Scripture. Along similar lines, because Jesus constantly confused the Pharisees, He at one point asked them, "Why is my language not clear to you?" He immediately answered His own question, saying, "Because you are unable to hear what I say" (John 8:43, NIV).

Now, Jesus obviously wasn't saying that the Pharisees were deaf. Rather, Jesus was pointing out that these religious leaders were incapable of grasping His outward speech. As Jesus elsewhere taught, when "people's hearts become calloused; they hardly hear with their ears, and they have closed eyes" (Matthew 13:15, NIV).

Jesus's own disciples illustrate the truth of this teaching. At one point Jesus said, "Destroy this temple, and I will raise it again in three days." John tells us that people thought He was talking about the temple in Jerusalem, but He was actually referring to His own body. Then John adds, "After He was raised from the dead, His disciples recalled what He had said. Then they believed the scripture and the words that Jesus had spoken" (John 2:19, 22, NIV).

Only after Jesus's resurrection did the disciples believe that He fulfilled all Scripture or the words He had spoken. See, like most Jews of the time, Jesus's disciples expected a victorious military Messiah. So when Jesus started talking about His need to go to Jerusalem to be arrested, beaten, and killed, it went in one ear and out the other. Peter once objected to this sort of talk, but even he forgot about it (see Matthew 16:21-22). For when Jesus was arrested, beaten, and killed, just as He said, they were totally shocked! And when Jesus rose from the dead, just as He had said He would, they were, initially, even more shocked! Only when the dust had settled and their eyes had been opened could they recall what Jesus had been telling them all along.

JESUS IS THE IMAGE OF THE INVISIBLE GOD

In contrast to many teachings regarding the character and nature of God, especially portrayed through the violent and vengeful imagery in the Old Testament, it's essential to recognize that Janus, the two-faced Roman god, does not represent our loving heavenly Father.

God has a singular face, revealed through Jesus. In Jesus, we see the Father's likeness, and in the Father, we see Jesus's reflection. This truth has always defined the essence of God.

"Whoever has seen Me has seen the Father" (John 14:9).

"No one can come to Me unless the Father who sent Me draws him" (John 6:44).

It is we who exhibit double-mindedness, not the divine Trinity. Presuming that God shares our dualistic and conflicting nature says more about our own characteristics than it does about His.

Janus: The Two-Faced Roman God

In the depths of Scripture, a profound revelation unfolds: the Father is unmistakably manifest in the person of Jesus Christ. Jesus Himself declared, "Whoever has seen Me, has seen the Father" (John 14:9). The book of Hebrews echoes this truth, affirming that in these last days, God speaks to us through His Son, who serves as the exact representation of His nature (see Hebrews 1:1-3). It's in Jesus that the divine voice finds its clearest resonance.

Contrary to misconceptions, Jesus doesn't stand opposed to the God revealed in the old covenant; rather, He embodies the purest revelation of that very God. Jesus has lifted the veil that once shrouded our understanding of the Father, offering clarity and unity. He doesn't wage war against the Father's will; rather, He reflects it perfectly. Yet, misinterpretations persist, leading some to believe in a Jesus who intervenes to shield us from the wrath of a distant and indifferent God. Such notions distort the essence of Christ's message and have seeped into the fabric of religious thought for generations.

The New Testament urges us to anchor our understanding of God in the person of Jesus. He is not merely a prophet among many; He is the ultimate revelation of God's character and nature. Even the laws and teachings of the Old Testament, once seen as shadows, find their fulfillment and truth in Christ. Once the pure and bright light of the Person of Jesus illuminates the shadowed images of God, we will then discover God has always been life, light, and love.

Jesus's own words bear witness to His unique stature as the revealer of God. He claimed a testimony greater than that of John the Baptist, surpassing all who came before Him. In His teachings, He overturned age-old laws, replacing them with the radical call to love and forgiveness. In doing so, He not only revealed God's true nature but also reshaped the very foundations of justice. Jesus exemplified that justice devoid of love merely amounts to vengeance. True justice, stemming from God's heart, surpasses mere retribution or retaliatory measures. Divine justice always carries the essence of restoration. It didn't matter how pure and true the gospel of Jesus was, it was humanity's thirst for vengeance that led to the crucifixion of the Son of God.

The New Testament directs us to focus our understanding of God on Jesus. Unlike past communications from God, the writer of Hebrews declares that Jesus is the exclusive "exact representation of God's being" (Hebrews 1:3, NIV). He is referred to as the Word of God (see John 1:1) and the image of God (see Colossians 1:15). When Philip asked Jesus to reveal God the Father, Jesus replied, "If you see me, you see the Father. Why do you ask to see the Father?" (John 14:7-9, author paraphrase). Even John 1:17-18 indicates that true knowledge of God comes only through Jesus. Therefore, Paul and the author of Hebrews depict the law and other elements of the Old Testament as mere shadows, with Christ alone being the reality (see Colossians 2; Hebrews 8; 10).

JESUS IS THE BRIDGE THAT HELPS US GET TO THE HEART OF GOD'S LOVE AND GRACE, GOING WAY BEYOND WHAT WE CAN GRASP ON OUR OWN.

Colossians 1:15 describes Jesus as "the image of the invisible God, the firstborn over all creation." Jesus Himself claimed to have a testimony greater than that of John the Baptist (see John 5), despite acknowledging John's greatness as a prophet before Him (see Matthew 11). This suggests that Jesus's revelation supersedes everything that came before Him. He even stated that true knowledge of God is exclusively through Him and those to whom

He reveals God (see Matthew 11:27), which includes all Old Testament authors.

This explains why Jesus felt empowered to challenge certain aspects of Old Testament revelation. For instance, He replaced the Old Testament law of "an eye for an eye" (found three times in the Old Testament) with His command to turn the other cheek and love your enemies (see Matthew 5:39, 44). What's intriguing is that the "eye for an eye" law, known as lex talionis, forms the bedrock of Old Testament justice. Jesus challenged the very foundation of Old Testament justice itself when He overturned this principle!

When we look at Jesus, the curtains are finally pulled back, revealing the whole picture of who God is and how to really understand what He's all about. Jesus is the bridge that helps us get to the heart of God's love and grace, going way beyond what we can grasp on our own.

CHAPTER 2

GOD STAYED SILENT

> *"When you did these things and I kept silent,*
> *you thought I was exactly like you."*
> —Psalm 50:21 (NIV)

> *"The way a person imagines and experiences God says at least as much about that person as it does God. The more estranged people are from God, the more their knowledge of him is obstructed and distorted. And when people yield to the Spirit, they are empowered to discern the true glory of God 'in the face of Jesus Christ.'"*
> —Greg Boyd[6]

In the Psalms, you can often tell if the writer is feeling spiritually uplifted or deeply troubled. By looking at how a psalm starts, you can see where God's help is needed to address the truths expressed in the song. For instance, phrases like "My God, my God, why have You forsaken me" (Psalm 22:1, NIV) or "Lord, do not rebuke me in your anger" (Psalm 6:1, NIV) show distress, while "How long, LORD? Will you forget me forever?"

---

6 Greg Boyd, "The God Who Stoops," *ReKnew*, 25 Apr. 2017, reknew.org/2017/04/the-god-who-stoops/.

(Psalm 13:1, NIV) expresses longing for God's presence. These songs are not usually sung in church because we prefer uplifting anthems over somber tunes. Nevertheless, it's important to study and appreciate the somber tones and themes of the Psalms. They offer insights into the challenges humanity encounters and reveal a redemptive thread, demonstrating the unwavering presence of a compassionate Father who refuses to abandon us in our darkest moments.

> **WHY DO WE FEEL THE NEED TO RESHAPE GOD IN OUR OWN IMAGE IF WE'RE ALREADY CONTENT WITH OURSELVES?**

In recent years, I've found Psalm 50 to be especially intriguing among the various instances where the Spirit of God influences the songwriting of different psalmists. Credited to Asaph, a prominent figure in the musical leadership of King David's tabernacle, this psalm initiates with a compelling summons for all to focus on the profound reverence owed to God. As the verses unfold, we witness a prophetic outpouring directly from the heart of God. From verse 17 onward, God lists a series of human behaviors starkly contrasting with His own character and nature. These include disdain for His teachings, complicity with thieves, engagement in adultery, propagation of deceit and malice through speech, and the spiteful defamation of one's own kin. As we reach verse 21, we find that despite the catalog of ungodly behaviors listed, God chose to remain silent.

Before we can contemplate the significance of God's silence, He clarifies the reason behind it: He remained silent because we mistakenly believed He was exactly like us. Why does it seem to be the instinctive response of human reasoning to interpret God's silence as passive endorsement of our actions? It's a question worth exploring. Perhaps it stems from the deeply ingrained tendency to create God in our own image—a deity who mirrors our appearance, echoes our beliefs, and even aligns with our political views. Throughout much of human history, we've fashioned a "god" who resembles us in every way. In this context, when faced with divine silence, we may unconsciously assume that God shares our perspectives and approves of our conduct. It's a reflection of our innate desire for affirmation and validation, a notion that if we're comfortable with our actions, surely God must be too. But such a limited understanding fails to grasp the true nature of the divine. So, why do we feel the need to reshape God in our own image if we're already content with ourselves?

No matter how real our projected images of God might appear, these images must fully submit to the self-sacrificial other-centered love that Jesus demonstrates in and through His earthly ministry.

A SHIFT IN PERSPECTIVE

In the narrative of Scripture, apart from the focus on Jesus and the New Testament's exploration of His ministry, some instances within the Old Testament give us a profound understanding of God's nature. These early passages offer rich insights into God's character. God initiates personal revelation and connectedness with various individuals throughout this period. Consider a few examples: Firstly, God reveals His goodness through the act of creation itself. Secondly, despite Adam and Eve's disobedience, God pursues them with compassion. Thirdly, individuals such as Abraham and Noah are deemed righteous based solely on their faith.

However, a drastic shift in the portrayal of God's nature occurs as the narrative progresses to Exodus 19. Here, for the first time in human history, people demand a mediator between themselves and God (see Exodus 20:18-21). This demand alters the dynamic of God's interaction with humanity and serves as one of the great literary crucifixes we have witnessed in human history. The legalistic demands of the nation of Israel create a lens through which they begin to behold "Rorschach Imagery" of a once loving and merciful Father.

The Godhead appears to assume the role of the enforcer of this demanded covenant from Israel. It's crucial to understand that the purpose of the law was never meant to facilitate a direct relationship between humanity and God but rather to expose sin and illuminate humanity's need for divine intervention. The law, therefore, is sin-focused (see 1 Corinthians 15:56), lacking in faith (see Galatians 3:12), and ultimately the administration of death (see 2 Corinthians 3:7).

Over time, God grew weary of the very people He deeply loved misinterpreting Him, misrepresenting Him, and perceiving Him as a harsh judge. Consequently, God chose to remain silent for four hundred years, signaling a period of divine quiet. The divine silence mentioned wasn't a literal absence of His Word, as such silence would imply the dissolution of all existence (see Psalm 33:6; Hebrews 11:3). Rather, it symbolizes God's intention to reset humanity's perception of His character and reaffirm His true essence—a God who is eternally loving and merciful.

PERCEPTIONS OF GOD < NATURE OF GOD

Before we explore a few of these Bible stories more deeply to search out the character and nature of God, it's worth reflecting on the relatively narrow scope of the Scriptural narrative, particularly as presented in the Old Testament. While the events described in Exodus 19 are commonly estimated to have occurred around 3,500 years ago, it's important to acknowledge that this timeframe doesn't encompass the entirety of human history or global civilizations. For instance, ancient Chinese civilization has been traced back to at least five thousand years through extensive archaeological evidence and cultural development.

This contrast prompts us to consider broader questions beyond the confines of the scriptural narrative. How did God interact with people in other regions, such as the oriental civilizations, during this era? Did they perceive divine intervention and guidance in ways similar to the Israelites, or did their cultural context shape different interpretations of the divine? Exploring these inquiries opens up fascinating avenues for understanding the diverse ways in which humanity has engaged with spirituality throughout history.

IF THERE'S ANYTHING YOU BELIEVE ABOUT GOD THAT DOESN'T LOOK LIKE JESUS, YOU'RE MISSING SOMETHING.

Throughout the Old Testament, numerous instances showcase the authentic character and nature of God. A useful guideline for discerning a more accurate depiction of the eternally loving and merciful God is to align perceptions with the portrayal of Jesus. If any aspect attributed to God in the Scriptures appears inconsistent with Jesus's compassionate and merciful nature, it suggests a potential misunderstanding or oversight. In short, if there's anything you believe about God that doesn't look like Jesus, you're missing something.

This principle underscores the importance of viewing the Old Testament through the lens of Jesus's teachings and actions. Jesus serves as the ultimate revelation of God's character, offering a tangible example of love, compassion, and forgiveness. By comparing depictions of God in the Old Testament with Jesus's compassionate and merciful nature, we can deepen our understanding of God's consistent and unwavering character across both testaments of the Bible.

One of the foundational stories that warrants careful examination is found in the Genesis account—the story of Adam and Eve. This narrative is likely familiar to many from childhood Sunday School lessons. However, upon closer inspection, one might ponder why God didn't respond with greater severity to their transgression. After all, they were responsible for introducing sin into the world. It might seem logical to expect God to unleash His full wrath upon them. Yet, surprisingly, God's response was not one of immediate punishment but of compassion. Instead of distancing Himself from Adam and Eve, God swiftly approached them, offering multiple opportunities for repentance.

In this context, repentance wasn't solely about acknowledging wrongdoing; it was also about reconsidering their imaging of God. Adam and Eve had succumbed to the deception that God was withholding something from them, perpetuating a false belief that God was a restrictive force. This flawed perspective had taken root deeply within them, influencing their understanding of God's character and intentions. Therefore, God's actions aimed not only to address their actions but also to challenge and transform their flawed perception of Him.

Another aspect of the story of Adam and Eve that unveils the true character and nature of God is seen when they become aware of their nakedness. In Genesis 3:21, it's God who provides a sacrifice to clothe them. Remarkably, God doesn't require Adam and Eve to provide their own sacrifice to cover their sin; instead, He graciously provides it for them. This gesture underscores a fundamental aspect of God's nature: He is a giver, not a taker. Throughout the biblical narrative, this theme remains consistent—God's inclination is always towards giving, whether it be provision, mercy, or redemption. This act of grace from the very beginning of humanity exemplifies the essence of who God truly is—an ever-loving and generous provider.

It is widely accepted that the fundamental root of sin is pride, often referred to as the "original sin." However, the immediate consequence of sin, as Adam and Eve experienced, is their sense of original shame. In that crucial moment, instead of mocking or belittling them, God responds with love and compassion by covering them.

What we call Original Sin in Genesis perhaps could, in a sense, be better called Original Shame, because Adam

> and Eve describe themselves as feeling naked. Some of the first words of God to these newly created people are, "Who told you that you were naked?" (Genesis 3:11). Next, in a lovely maternal image, God as seamstress sews leather garments for them (see 3:21). The first thing God does after creation itself is cover the shame of these new creatures.[7]

The ancient narrative of Abraham and Isaac offers another profound insight into the true character and nature of God. In this story, Abraham finds himself in a remarkable encounter with the divine—or at least what appears to be a deity, from Abraham's perspective. Astonishingly, it doesn't take long for the unsettling demand for human sacrifice to emerge (see Genesis 22:2).

It's essential to consider Abraham's background. He hails from Ur, a land steeped in idolatry, where the prevailing gods were often portrayed as capricious and bloodthirsty. This cultural backdrop likely shapes Abraham's perception of divine beings. Thus, when confronted with what he believes to be God's command to sacrifice his beloved son, Isaac, Abraham's reaction is surprisingly subdued. There's little indication of protest, despite the apparent contradiction of sacrificing the very son whom God had promised to him.

In the pivotal moment of the story, Abraham, with a knife poised to carry out the unthinkable act of sacrificing his own son, is wholly committed to fulfilling what he believes to be God's command. Yet, just as Abraham is about to commit the irreparable deed, God intervenes, halting him in his tracks. This dramatic

---

[7] Richard Rohr, *The Wisdom Pattern: Order, Disorder, Reorder* (Cincinnati, OH: Franciscan Media, May 1, 2020).

turn of events echoes the character of the God we encountered earlier in Genesis—a God who, rather than demanding sacrifice from Adam and Eve in their moment of shame, provided them with coverings. Indeed, God Himself provided the sacrificial lamb (see Genesis 22:8), reaffirming that God is always a giver, never a taker.

IN ASSUMING THE DISTORTED IMAGING OF ABRAHAM'S LANGUAGE AND CULTURAL CONTEXT, GOD CONFRONTS THE WIDELY ACCEPTED NOTION OF HUMAN SACRIFICE, TAKING IT TO ITS EXTREME IN THE NARRATIVE ATOP MOUNT MORIAH.

This "come to God" moment marks a significant revelation for Abraham. In it, he discovers a new aspect of God's character—a name: *Jehovah Jireh*, the Provider. This name encapsulates the essence of God's nature as One who abundantly provides for His people, even in the most dire circumstances. It serves as a powerful reminder that God's love and provision extend beyond what we can fathom, offering hope and reassurance in times of uncertainty.

We are prompted to ask a crucial question when we examine this encounter through the lens of "Rorschach Imagery" that Abraham's cultural experiences influenced: did God truly command Abraham to sacrifice his son, Isaac? From my perspective,

I contend that Abraham genuinely believed that God had issued this command, but his cultural experiences shaped his belief and were then projected onto his ideas concerning the behavior and desires of "deities." In assuming the distorted imaging of Abraham's language and cultural context, God confronts the widely accepted notion of human sacrifice, taking it to its extreme in the narrative atop Mount Moriah. Through this dramatic scenario, God unveils His authentic character and nature to Abraham, who would later be revered as the father of faith (see Galatians 3:6-9). Crucially, throughout history, God has never been a taker nor has He ever desired human sacrifice. Instead, He consistently demonstrates His faithfulness and provision. This narrative underscores the eternal trustworthiness of God. He will not take your laughter!

> *The real tragedy here is that God, man's benevolent, triune, familial Creator, was perceived as being on an equal level with the pagan gods of antiquity—selfish gods who had no problem with taking the life of your loved one in order to satisfy their own needs. Abraham, while a Godly man, had yet to have his mind fully purged of the pagan notions that had been ingrained in him in his native Ur, and God, while patient with Abraham's misunderstandings, was not content to let them go unchallenged.*[8]

We now turn our attention to the epic tale of Noah's flood for this chapter's final example and exploration of the re-imaging of God's character and nature. While you may be familiar with the story of Noah, let's revisit its origins to fully grasp its significance.

---

[8] Jeff Turner, *Saints in the Arms of a Happy God: Recovering the Image of God and Man* (Jeff Turner, April 16, 2014).

At the outset, God observes the pervasive wickedness in the world and decides to take action. He singles out righteous Noah, declaring, "I am going to put an end to all people, for the earth is filled with violence because of them. I am surely going to destroy both them and the earth" (Genesis 6:13, NIV). God then provides Noah with detailed instructions: to construct an ark, gather pairs of animals of every kind, and stockpile provisions for the journey ahead, essentially initiating a fresh start akin to another genesis with Noah and his family. God was going to destroy the world with a flood.

As the rains poured down relentlessly for forty days and nights, the deluge engulfed the earth and wiped out all living creatures. Only Noah, his family, and the animals sheltered within the ark survived the cataclysmic event. The harrowing details of this ordeal are chronicled in Genesis 7-8.

It's important to acknowledge the longstanding scholarly debates surrounding Noah's flood narrative, including questions about its literal interpretation, the global or local extent of the flood, and its potential relationship with the *Epic of Gilgamesh*. Both the *Epic of Gilgamesh* and the Hebrew Scriptures originated from oral storytelling traditions, although certain fragments of the *Epic of Gilgamesh* that are in written form predate the Noah account in the Hebrew Scriptures.

One prevailing theory suggests the possibility of cultural borrowing, wherein the Israelites incorporated elements of the *Epic of Gilgamesh* into their own narrative to convey theological truths. While the *Epic of Gilgamesh* focuses on the pursuit of wisdom and the quest for immortality, the Noah story in the

Hebrew Scriptures emphasizes faith and trust in God amidst impending catastrophe.

In this light, the Noah narrative could be viewed as a deliberate reworking of earlier cultural motifs to serve a distinct theological purpose. By adapting and repurposing the flood motif, the Israelites may have sought to impart lessons about divine providence, human frailty, and the importance of fidelity to God's will. With that in mind, the aspect of the narrative that warrants direct consideration is whether God was both the cause of the flood and the savior of Noah and his family via the ark. If this notion holds true, can such a God be deemed trustworthy? These are undeniably weighty questions to grapple with.

Alternatively, if we interpret the story of Noah's flood literally, could it be that either Noah himself or, more likely, those transmitting the story through oral tradition over generations projected the feelings of revulsion and desire to cleanse humanity from the earth onto God? As you ponder this question, consider whether the God depicted in Noah's flood resembles Jesus more as the initiator of a catastrophic deluge or as the compassionate Savior who rescues from the tempest. I would submit that God cannot simultaneously embody both roles and still maintain His identity as an unconditionally loving, infinitely merciful, and unfailingly trustworthy Father.

RORSCHACH IMAGES ABOUND

Across the body of human history, the thirst for power has been a driving force, compelling individuals to seek dominion over others or, at the very least, to resist subjection to the rule of others. Given that men have historically held sway over religious institutions, it's hardly surprising that the concept of divine authority has often been intertwined with the desire for earthly power. This association persists despite the explicit directive in the dominion mandate outlined in Genesis 1:26-28, which delineates humanity's authority over creation rather than over fellow humans. The mandate emphasizes stewardship over the natural world, granting humans the responsibility to care for and cultivate the earth, rather than to exert dominance over one another. However, the historical fusion of religious and political authority has led to a pervasive misconception that the power to govern others is an inherent attribute of God or the gods. This misunderstanding has perpetuated systems of control and oppression throughout human civilization, often under the guise of divine sanction.

As this transactional arrangement takes root, it alters our perception of God. Distorted and fearful depictions of God obscure and replace the image of a gracious, merciful, and loving deity. The initial promise of intimacy gives way to a more rigid and distant understanding of the divine-human relationship. This divergence sets the stage for the gradual emergence of images of a severe, judgmental, and wrathful God.

By contrast, Paul's redefinition of the power of God, emphasizing self-sacrificial love exemplified on the seemingly weak instrument of the cross (see 1 Corinthians 1:18, 30), stands as a testament to the divine origin of his message. It's a message so radically different from conventional human wisdom that its source couldn't possibly be merely human invention. Indeed, this portrayal starkly contrasts with the coercive power historically attributed to God, a perception that has unfortunately persisted throughout much of church history.

> **THE HUMAN PROPENSITY TO MOLD GOD IN THEIR OWN FLAWED IMAGE OFTEN LED TO DISTORTED REPRESENTATIONS.**

Considering the Old Testament context, rife with the stubbornness and limited understanding of God's people, it's not surprising to find instances where God is depicted in ways that seem distorted or twisted. The human propensity to mold God in their own flawed image often led to distorted representations. However, what is truly remarkable is the presence of numerous depictions that align with the crucified Christ, revealing the Spirit of Christ breaking through the cultural and fallen mindset of the Israelites.

To truly grasp the extent of the ancient Israelites' distorted perception of God, take a moment to ponder a passage that may have gone unnoticed until viewing Scripture through the lens of the cross. In their efforts to persuade Pharaoh to release the Israelites, Aaron makes a striking statement: "The God of the Hebrews has met with us. Now let us take a three-day journey into the wilderness to offer sacrifices to the LORD our God, or he may strike us with plagues or with the sword" (Exodus 5:3, NIV).

There is no documentation of God issuing such a peculiar threat to Moses and Aaron. Moreover, it remains unclear why Moses and Aaron proposed only a three-day respite in the wilderness for worship when God had clearly communicated His desire for the Israelites to leave Egypt permanently. Equally puzzling is the rationale behind Moses and Aaron's belief that sacrifices to God necessitated a journey into the desert.

Moses and Aaron felt the weight of responsibility to persuade Pharaoh, believing that if they failed, God might punish them, and possibly all the Israelites, with "plagues or with the sword." This placed immense pressure on them, akin to burdening your sales representatives with an overwhelming task. Somewhere along the lines of communication between God and Moses/Aaron, there appears to have been a misunderstanding or distortion.

Let's pose an honest question. Who more closely embodies the character portrayed in this depiction of God: Jesus Christ or Al Capone? The answer is evident. Interestingly, we don't need to search extensively to discern the origin of this Al Capone-esque version of God that Moses and Aaron seem to have adopted. Throughout the Ancient Near East (ANE), we encounter instances where individuals attribute Al Capone-like threats to various gods.

Yet, there's a silver lining to be found in the preservation of this distorted and culturally influenced portrayal of God within the written accounts of our divine missionary's endeavors. It serves as a testament to the depths to which God was willing to descend to continue advancing His purposes throughout history via this particular group of people. This is how a stiff-necked and spiritually distorted people perceived God. And rather than forcibly implanting accurate mental images of Himself, God chose to leave these twisted perceptions intact as He graciously breathed life into the biblical narrative through them. In essence, this suggests that God had to be willing to shoulder the burden of the sinful and distorted projected images humanity held of Him, thereby assuming a distorted appearance that is still allowed or "breathed" into the scriptural record.

Again, the most profound transformation in humanity's perception and interaction with the divine unfolds in the narrative of Exodus 19. At its core, this passage illustrates God's beautiful offer of relational closeness to the Israelites, as articulated in Exodus 19:5-6. However, what follows is a pivotal moment where this offer is met with hesitation and fear, leading ultimately to rejection, as seen in Exodus 20:18-21. Instead of embracing the opportunity for direct intimacy with the divine, the people opt for a more transactional dynamic. They request a mediator and the establishment of a covenant—an agreement with clear terms—between themselves and God. This shift marks a significant departure from the initial invitation to relational closeness. It introduces a radical layer of separation, veiling direct encounters with God.

In essence, Exodus 19 presents a crucial turning point in the evolution of humanity's conception of God. It underscores the tension between the desire for intimacy and the inclination towards transactional arrangements in our relationship with the divine. Moreover, it highlights the consequences of veiling the face of God, as it paves the way for the emergence of distorted and unsettling depictions of the divine nature.

As the narratives of the Old Testament unfold, we encounter numerous instances of violence, either directly attributed to God Himself (see Numbers 16:49; 1 Samuel 2:25, 4:11) or commanded by Him through the actions of others (see Job 1:18-19; 1 Chronicles 5:18-22). The sheer amount of such violent examples is significant enough to warrant its own separate volume. When all is said and done, within the biblical narrative, God is associated with either directly causing or commanding the deaths of nearly three million people. It's important to note that this estimate does not even include the account of Noah's flood!

> **THE MOSAIC LAW, RATHER THAN CLARIFYING THE AUTHENTIC NATURE OF GOD, SEEMED TO CONTRIBUTE TO ITS FURTHER DISTORTION.**

In addition to the violence that we've briefly examined, the most deeply disturbing and twisted depictions of God emerge in the crucifixion of His only begotten Son, Jesus. Here we witness the sacrifice of the righteous, sinless Son who takes upon Himself the punishment intended for all humanity. The crucifixion of Jesus appears to be a profound paradox that challenges our understanding of justice, mercy, and the nature of God Himself. It begs the unsettling questions: How can we reconcile worshiping and placing our trust in a God who appears bloodthirsty, willing to offer up the innocent to save the guilty? How can such a God be trustworthy?

Now, we're beginning to grasp the extent to which the interpretations of God's character became increasingly ambiguous and subjective. The Mosaic law, rather than clarifying the authentic nature of God, seemed to contribute to its further distortion. It's no surprise then, that prior to the arrival of Jesus in the Gospels, there's a sense of God's silence. Can we really blame Him? What will it take to restore the image of God to accurately reflect His true character—an eternally merciful, gracious, self-sacrificial Father, whose essence is centered on others? The solution will require a paradigm shift that humanity never saw coming.

CHAPTER 3

THE ROLE OF SCRIPTURE

"The Bible in itself is not the Word of God. The Word of God is a person (John 1:1). Neither does the Bible have life, power or light in itself any more than did the Jewish Torah. These attributes may be ascribed to the Bible only by virtue of its relationship to Him who is Word, Life, Power and Light. Life is not in the book, as the Pharisees supposed, but only in the Man of the book (John 5:39)."
—Robert Brinsmead[9]

At this juncture, it's wise to wrestle with the intended purpose of Scripture. Undoubtedly, as you've engaged with its contents, you may have encountered inquiries such as, "Does the Bible contain inaccuracies?" or "Are there elements within it that lack truth?" or even, "If certain verses appear questionable, how can I discern the trustworthy ones?" These are all legitimate questions, and in the forthcoming chapter, I aim to present what I believe are constructive methods to approach, interpret, and glean from Scripture in accordance with its original intent for us.

---

9 "A Freedom from Biblicalism" in *The Christian Verdict*, Essay 14, 1984. Fallbrook: Verdict Publications, 9-14)

There's a long-standing observation that has humorously circulated in conservative circles, particularly in the South, although its reach likely extends beyond our region. It goes something like this: the Holy Trinity consists of the Father, Son, and Holy Bible. While often uttered in jest, there's a nugget of truth to it. Over time, we've elevated Scripture to the status of deity, granting it power and authority that it was never intended to possess. The Scriptures serve as a guide to lead us to Christ, the Living Word of God, from whom we receive our spiritual life.

Paul contrasted the letter of the law with the Spirit in his second epistle to the Corinthian church, as he wrote:

> *Not that we are competent in ourselves to claim anything for ourselves, but our competence comes from God. He has made us competent as ministers of a new covenant— not of the letter but of the Spirit; for the letter kills, but the Spirit gives life.* —2 Corinthians 3:5-6 (NIV)

THREE METHODS FOR APPROACHING SCRIPTURE

Biblical Inerrancy: The Weakest Way

The initial approach to Scripture that I'll discuss, I contend, is the most recent, weakest, and regrettably, the most prevalent in Western reading and teaching. This method is known as biblical inerrancy. Biblical inerrancy is the belief some Christians hold that the Bible, in its original manuscripts, is without error or fault in all matters it addresses—whether theological, historical, scientific, or otherwise. This belief asserts that the Bible is completely accurate and trustworthy in all its teachings and assertions. Adherents to biblical inerrancy typically hold that the Holy Spirit guided the authors of the Bible to ensure that what they wrote was free from error. This belief often extends to the idea that translations and copies of the original manuscripts, when done faithfully, maintain this inerrancy. This method of interpreting Scripture leads some to uphold beliefs like "young earth" creationism, despite substantial evidence suggesting the Earth is much older than 6,000 years. It also maintains the view that Noah's flood was a literal global event, requiring all animals to be present on the ark for survival. Additionally, adherents may insist that the blood flow mentioned in Revelation 14:20 must reach the level of a horse's bridle literally. There are many other examples available, but you get the idea.

BIBLICAL INERRANCY SOMETIMES LEADS US TO IMPOSE EXPECTATIONS ON SCRIPTURE THAT IT WAS NOT ORIGINALLY INTENDED TO FULFILL.

Biblical inerrancy sometimes leads us to impose expectations on Scripture that it was not originally intended to fulfill. For instance, Scripture isn't primarily focused on detailing the extensive histories of civilizations beyond the ancient Israelites and the nations directly involved in the biblical narrative. The Bible, when viewed as a history book, primarily focuses on the ancient Near East, making it less comprehensive as a historical record if one's scope extends beyond this region. Similarly, it doesn't deeply explore scientific explanations or the mechanics of the universe. This is evident in stories like the Tower of Babel in Genesis 11, where considerations such as altitude could have halted the project, or in the account of the sun standing still in Joshua 10, which contradicts our modern understanding of the Earth's rotation around the sun.

In addition to numerous examples illustrating why biblical inerrancy may not be a beneficial approach to Scripture, it also diverges from the rich storytelling tradition of Eastern philosophy. It's important to remember that the Bible, with its myriad stories, originates from the East. It would also greatly benefit Westerners to engage in studies on the lifestyles and perspectives of the people depicted in the historical narratives of the Bible. The Western inclination towards an inerrant lens closely aligned with the sin of certainty has led to a significant departure from the storytelling ethos characteristic of Eastern traditions.

There also exist numerous factual discrepancies within the Scriptures. However, if we approach Scripture with the expectation of factual accuracy, then there is little room to accommodate such errors. Consider a straightforward example: when did Mary Magdalene first discover the empty tomb? According to Mark 16:2, it was after sunrise, yet John 20:1 suggests it was still dark. Furthermore, John indicates that she observed the stone had already been removed while it was dark, whereas Mark portrays her arriving at the tomb after sunrise, pondering who would remove the stone for her. Any attempt to reconcile these accounts may only serve to exacerbate the apparent contradictions.

Beyond its tendency to assign purposes to Scripture that it was never meant to fulfill, an inerrant approach compels readers to defend perceived inaccuracies regardless of historical, scientific, or theological contradictions. This has led to the emergence of the Christian Apologetics movement. While this movement has contributed positively to Western culture's inclination towards intellectual reasoning and empirical evidence, it can also be detrimental. The Scriptures prioritize communicating profound, mystical truths over intellectualism, where logic often fails to grasp its essence.

Lastly, concerning our focus in this section of the chapter, advocates of biblical inerrancy seek a Bible devoid of human errors (acknowledging humanity's propensity for mistakes), yet their very premise exposes a contradiction. Fallible individuals are tasked with discerning the Bible's assertions. Humans, prone to error, must engage in the challenging task of interpretation. Imperfect beings are therefore responsible for discerning the significance and intent of Scripture.

The term "inerrancy" is problematic because, as Roger Olson (American theologian and professor) observes, its definition is subject to numerous qualifications, leading to what he describes as "the death of a thousand qualifications."[10] Others use the term "inerrant" and do not mean "without errors," but rather "without errors when interpreted correctly." While it would be convenient to assume that Christians from various cultural backgrounds would all interpret the Bible in the same manner, such an assumption is untrue. Since the early days of the church, and particularly

---

10 Roger Olson, "Why inerrancy doesn't matter" https://www.patheos.com/blogs/rogereolson/2010/08/why-inerrancy-doesnt-matter/

since the Protestant Reformation, Christians have disagreed on the correct interpretation of the Bible, a phenomenon known as "pervasive interpretive pluralism."

Biblical Authority: It's Authoritative . . . When It's Authoritative

Biblical authority is the next approach to Scripture that we will take some time to examine. This view has more credibility than biblical inerrancy, but we must still be careful that we do not give equal authority to all Scripture simply because it's in the Bible. To say that Scripture is authoritative suggests that the Bible is considered important and helpful in guiding Christian practices because it's seen as God's Word. It involves evaluating the Bible and its sources to ensure its accuracy and importance in conveying God's message. This evaluation helps to guide how people practice their faith. Critical interpretation, called exegesis, and the science of interpretive principles, called hermeneutics, are used to determine biblical authority.

> **I'VE NEVER MET ANYONE WHO BELIEVES THAT EVERY PART OF THE BIBLE CARRIES EQUAL AUTHORITY.**

Truthfully, I've never met anyone who believes that every part of the Bible carries equal authority. If someone did hold that belief, they'd be advocating for practices like stoning disobedient children (see Deuteronomy 21:18-21), refraining from cutting their hair or shaving (see Leviticus 19:27), and remaining uncircumcised, risking exclusion from their community (see Genesis 17:14). Now, you might argue, "Those are clearly antiquated ceremonial laws and are irrelevant today." I agree, but what about a few more examples from the New Testament? Should women cut off their hair if their head isn't covered (see 1 Corinthians 11:6) or remain silent in church (see 1 Corinthians 14) or avoid hairstyling or braiding (see 1 Peter 3:3)? You might counter, "Those were cultural norms for that time," or "these passages are being misinterpreted." This is why the authority of Scripture can quickly become a difficult conversation to have.

While the question of biblical authority might appear unimportant, there are aspects of it that carry significant weight. Consider, for instance, how Scriptures were employed to justify slavery in the southern states. Despite the Bible containing hundreds of thousands of words, southern slaveholders—many of whom identified themselves as Christian—relied heavily on two specific passages. These passages, one from the beginning of the Old Testament and the other from the New Testament, were Genesis 9:18-27 and Ephesians 6:5-7. They were utilized to construct the fallacious concept of "the curse of Ham," associating Africans with Noah's son and purportedly justifying their subjugation.

Pro-slavery advocates frequently searched the Old Testament for examples to support their position, citing instances where slavery was prevalent among the Israelites. Conversely, they largely disregarded the New Testament, except to note the absence of Jesus's condemnation of slavery. However, they often referenced the story of Philemon, where St. Paul returned a runaway slave to his master. Additionally, it was commonly believed that the Latin word *servus*, typically translated as "servant," actually meant "slave." Like it or not, numerous verses in the Bible appear to endorse slavery. However, the critical question remains: why would individuals use such verses to justify contemporary slavery? Sadly, it only requires one proof text to ignite the darkest recesses of a person's heart.

Reviewing the work of the bulk of southern white churches, Frederick Douglass had this to say:

> *Between the Christianity of this land and the Christianity of Christ, I recognize the widest possible difference—so wide that to receive the one as good, pure, and holy, is of necessity to reject the other as bad, corrupt, and wicked. To be the friend of the one is of necessity to be the enemy of the other. I love the pure, peaceable, and impartial Christianity of Christ; I therefore hate the corrupt, slave-holding, women-whipping, cradle-plundering, partial and hypocritical Christianity of this land. Indeed, I can see no reason but the most deceitful one for calling the religion of this land Christianity.*[11]

IF CERTAIN SCRIPTURES POSSESS AUTHORITY WHILE OTHERS DO NOT, BY WHAT CRITERIA OR PERSPECTIVE CAN WE DISCERN SUCH DIFFERENCES?

---

11 *Narrative of the Life of Fredrick Douglas*, Fredrick Douglas, 1845.

There are also compelling examples of the authority of Scripture worth examining. For instance, consider the beautiful encouragement in Galatians 6:2, urging us to bear one another's burdens and fulfill the law of Christ. Additionally, reflect on the profound depiction of love in 1 John 3:16 (NASB), which states, "We know love by this, that He laid down His life for us; and we ought to lay down our lives for the brothers and sisters." Furthermore, there are deeply mystical truths to contemplate, such as those found in Romans 5:18-21. These verses illustrate how one act of righteousness leads to justification and life for all, countering the effects of sin with the abundance of grace through Jesus Christ our Lord.

I suggest that we explore questions regarding which Scriptures hold authority and relevance for our lives. Are all Scriptures of equal importance? If certain Scriptures possess authority while others do not, by what criteria or perspective can we discern such differences? I believe these questions are more fruitful. They encourage a mindset of inquiry rather than seeking the certainty that analytical thinking demands. These questions foster an environment where faith can flourish, not by lacking in faith, but by cultivating an atmosphere conducive to its growth.

Biblical Inspiration: God Breathes (Inspired) the Scriptural Record

> *"Scripture is breathed by God not to function as a revelation in its own right, but to serve as a witness to the one revelation of the triune God in Jesus Christ."* —Karl Barth[12]

---
12 Barth, Karl. *Church Dogmatics*. Edited by G. W. Bromiley and T. F. Torrance. Translated by G. T. Thomson and Harold Knight. Vol. 1, *The Doctrine of the Word of God: Prolegomena to Church Dogmatics*. Edinburgh: T. & T. Clark, 1956.

Throughout history, the orthodox Christian tradition has affirmed that all canonical writings are "God-breathed" (2 Timothy 3:16, NIV). But what does this concept truly mean? How could God ensure that the writings produced through His "breathing" are precisely what they intended without compromising the autonomy of the writers whom He "breathed" through? In simpler terms, did God compel the authors to write exactly what they wrote?

To affirm that the Scriptures are inspired means to acknowledge that they are "God-breathed," or perhaps more precisely, that God "allowed" their recording in the form we have them. If we acknowledge that God "breathed" Scripture in the same way as He "breathed" Jesus, and if everything Jesus represented is closely tied to the cross, then I suggest that our comprehension of "God-breathed" Scripture should also be centered on the cross. Therefore, we need to reflect on how God's actions on Calvary might shape our understanding of His actions in Scripture.

I believe the most crucial aspect of God's revelation at Calvary is this: on Calvary, Jesus's actions toward humans not only clearly revealed God (which is always with goodness, kindness, patience, mercy, and love) but also allowed humans and the fallen powers to act upon Him (which is typically through violence). While God initiated the plan of salvation, which involved the Son of God incarnating at the opportune moment for His crucifixion, He also took the initiative as Jesus taught and acted in ways certain to lead to His crucifixion. Thus, Scripture states that part of God's deliberate plan and foreknowledge was to have Jesus handed over to wicked individuals to fulfill what was in God's heart all along (see Acts 2:23-24).

While God was actively engaged in His demonstrative action on Calvary, we must also recognize that this revelatory event occurred through God allowing wicked humans and forces of evil to carry out their violent intentions against Jesus. The physical and verbal assaults Jesus endured during His crucifixion reflected the sin of the world that He bore on the cross, allowing every human throughout history to impact Him. Within this interplay of action and reception, God communicates His true identity. Given that His true nature is humble and self-sacrificial, it's difficult to imagine it happening any other way. A powerful deity could've revealed Himself by only acting upon others, but not the one true triune God, whose eternal existence is a continuous exchange of love among three divine Persons.

I believe the cross stands as the complete revelation of God's character precisely because it wasn't solely an independent action of God towards humans, but rather, in part, emerged from God humbly permitting flawed humans to engage in hostile activities against Him. This paradigmatic act of communication wasn't just a demonstration of God's power, but also of His wisdom. Through His wisdom, God transformed the evil directed towards Him into good, including the revelation of His true self-sacrificial nature, the triumph over evil powers, and the liberation of humanity from the bondage of sin.

Considering the ideal act of a self-revelatory event at Calvary exemplifies the ultimate purpose of all divine expressions and garners recognition that this act involved both humanity acting upon God and God acting upon humanity, it becomes challenging not to apply this principle to all of God's acts of self-revelation. Embracing this notion fundamentally reshapes our understanding of the divine inspiration of Scripture. In essence, it suggests that our affirmation of Scripture as divinely inspired does not imply that everything within the canon stems solely from God acting through human authors. Reflecting the cruciform nature of God, these writings also capture God's humility in permitting the culturally conditioned and sin-influenced worldviews of biblical authors to impact Him. As God has perpetually sought a relational journey with humanity, the presence of flaws, inaccuracies, and "Rorschach Imagery" within the text makes the Bible even more captivating and relatable.

Additionally, like we witness in God's revelation on Calvary, Scripture's inspiration should not only be understood as a display of God's power but also as a reflection of His wisdom. Just as with the cross, we should anticipate that, in order to achieve His goals, God will incorporate the various ways in which He has allowed the imperfect perspectives of human authors to influence His message in Scripture.

The crucifixion illustrates the self-sacrificial, other-centered love of the triune God, revealing that this has always been Their essence. While certain images attributed to God may seem contrary to this nature, they are inaccurate when compared to His true character. We can understand these un-Christlike depictions as misrepresentations, akin to repeatedly crucifying God. However, it also demonstrates God's kindness and patience in bearing the burden of these projections, retaining them in the inspired Scriptures to emphasize His value for relational intimacy and disinterest in controlling what we believe about Him. In essence, the inspiration of Scripture shows us that while the Bible is God's story, He allows His children to write it.

Ava, my youngest daughter, will occasionally bring home artwork from a day well spent at school. I adore her excitement when she shows me a new picture born straight out of her blossoming creativity. On more than one occasion, while admiring a new piece of her work, I have asked, "Who is this in your picture?" And on more than one occasion, usually to my surprise, she answers, "That's you, Dad!" I love her drawing of me, even though it looks nothing like me. I celebrate her, even though the image has claws like a wolverine and a four-inch waistline. But I hang it on the fridge anyway because she's my daughter. I love her more than my own life. As she continues to mature, her ability to communicate who I am to others will become much richer and more authentic.

THE VALUE OF THE BIBLE LIES IN ITS ROLE AS GOD'S WORD, FAITHFULLY DIRECTING US TO THE LIVING WORD OF GOD, JESUS CHRIST.

THE JESUS HERMENEUTIC

Difficulties arise with the Bible when its primary purpose, that of guiding us to Jesus, is obscured. It is crucial to remember that the Bible is not the ultimate goal; it is neither God itself nor the focal point of our faith. Rather, Jesus is our ultimate aim, our God, in whom we place our trust. The value of the Bible lies in its role as God's word, faithfully directing us to the living Word of God, Jesus Christ. Forgetting this can lead us astray, even as we diligently study the Bible! Jesus Himself expressed this when He said, "You search the scriptures because you think that in them you have eternal life; and it is they that bear witness about me. Yet you refuse to come to me to have life" (John 5:39-40).

The Pharisees tragically made Scripture an end in itself, using it as proof texts to validate themselves and condemn others. They prioritized knowledge of the Scriptures over obeying God's will and used them as weapons against their enemies. Unfortunately, modern-day Pharisees often follow the same pattern. Emily Brontë, in her novel *Wuthering Heights*, describes an intolerable, judgmental Christian with this scathing sentence: "He was, and likely still is, the most tiresome, self-righteous Pharisee imaginable, who scoured the Bible to claim promises for himself and hurl curses at his neighbors." This observation by Brontë echoes the thoughts of Leo Tolstoy, who said, "People who claim to be Christians but do not live accordingly are the most dangerous enemies of Christianity."[13]

When we lose sight of the Bible's role in leading us to Jesus, we risk manipulating it to fit our desires. It becomes like a trained dog, obedient to our whims. With a concordance and a little ingenuity, we can cherry-pick passages to support our opinions in minutes. Proof-texting becomes a game, where almost anything can be "proved" using selective Bible verses. Wars, capital punishment, slavery, the subjugation of women, and ethnic cleansing have all been justified this way. But Jesus doesn't endorse any of these practices! If Christians don't interpret the Bible in the context of Christ's teachings, they might as well not read it at all.

For Christians, the first half of the Bible tells the inspired story leading to Jesus—the Word of God in human form. Along this

---
13 *The Kingdom of God is Within You*, 1927

journey, we see evolving perspectives that we should acknowledge. Practices like ritual sacrifice, violence, dietary laws, and cultural sanctions in God's name are all eventually reconsidered. The rituals of animal sacrifice, stoning Sabbath-breakers, and killing children are all part of the narrative leading to the Messiah's arrival. But once Jesus comes, everything must be seen in light of His teachings. Jesus rescues the Bible from being just another violent religious text. He brings a new perspective, preventing it from becoming merely violent and vengeful.

IT'S TRUE–THERE'S A HARMFUL WAY OF INTERPRETING THE BIBLE THAT STUNTS SPIRITUAL GROWTH.

Speaking of violent religious texts, Christians often criticize other religious texts, such as the Rig Veda, the Analects of Confucius, or the Quran, in the same way they could critique the Bible if interpreted in a certain manner. I know little about these other writings, but I'm aware that one can justify various atrocities by reading the Bible as a literal text, devoid of Christ's light. This is when the Bible becomes harmful. When it provides legalistic loopholes to avoid following Jesus's teachings in the Sermon on the Mount, it hinders genuine discipleship. It's true—there's a harmful way of interpreting the Bible that stunts spiritual growth.

Using Scriptural texts to create an echo chamber of confirmation bias always produces a god in our own image. If you're looking for a violent, punitive God, the Bible can certainly produce that. If you're seeking endorsement for capital punishment, you can find it in the Bible. If you want justification for hating or marginalizing your enemies, the Bible can provide that too. If you're looking for divine validation for every opinion you hold, the Bible can supply it. If you want to justify your pompous, self-righteous attitude, the Bible can accommodate that as well. If you want assurance that only those who believe just like you will enter heaven, the Bible can reassure you. When we interpret the Bible through our own flawed projections of God, we can manipulate its message to make it say almost anything, including our own biases and misconceptions about God.

Should your inclination be towards peace, nonviolence, mercy, forgiveness, reconciliation, humility, advocacy, and love, the Bible offers guidance in these virtues by consistently directing attention to Jesus. Approaching the Bible with altruistic intent reveals its message: "Focus on Jesus, for He embodies the true Word of God." When the Bible serves as a dependable roadmap leading to Jesus, it becomes beneficial. This marks the beginning of recognizing the consistent character and nature of God throughout the inspired record.

Answer this question for yourself: if you never encountered another Bible verse for the remainder of your life, could you still love and be loved by Jesus? The Bible should point us to Jesus, but it cannot be what we are ultimately rooted in. Beyond merely interpreting Scripture, Jesus desires to serve as the framework for every aspect of our lives. Jesus should shape and guide our actions and decisions. Our interactions with others should reflect the life and love of Jesus. Our efforts to heal and restore others should be rooted in the redemptive heart of Jesus.

Through the life and teachings of Jesus, we encounter the clear and distinct image of God. According to Jesus, the conclusion of the biblical story differs significantly from narratives portraying a violent God. While our projected images of the New Testament book of Revelation depict the world's end with a war of retribution resulting in the destruction of a third of God's children, Jesus presents a vision of the world's end as a grand banquet to which all of God's children are welcomed. These two contrasting images are irreconcilable. It's not a scenario of battle followed by a banquet; rather, they represent dramatically different perspectives.

For Christians, Jesus should stand as the ultimate revelation of God. He humanizes God's essence. Jesus unveils God's authentic nature to us through His words, "Be compassionate as your Father in heaven is compassionate" (Luke 6:36, author paraphrase). Jesus urges us to embrace radical living and love because that's the essence of God. Give generously, forgive boundlessly, and love unreservedly. Jesus's life testifies to a God of love and nonviolence who transcends labels of "good" and "bad."

Jesus had a radical approach to interpreting sacred texts, yet He deeply respected the Hebrew Bible, also known as the Old Testament. While His use of Scripture is evident in the Gospels, many Christians read the Bible differently without noticing. Following are several examples of Jesus's interpretive method:

Jesus didn't quote Scripture extensively, and He was criticized for it, as He taught with inner authority rather than like the scribes (see Mark 1:22).

He often spoke from His own experience of God and humanity, unlike the scribes and Pharisees who relied on case law from previous sources.

WHEN CHRISTIANS INSIST THAT EVERY LINE IN THE BIBLE HOLDS EQUAL IMPORTANCE OR AUTHORITY, THEY DIVERGE FROM JESUS'S APPROACH.

Jesus sometimes referenced non-Jewish or non-canonical sources, expanding beyond *sola Scriptura*. He even quoted sources seemingly inaccurately (see John 10:34).

While Jesus had a few favorite books like Exodus, Deuteronomy, Isaiah, Hosea, and Psalms, He ignored many others from His own Scriptures, especially those endorsing violence, imperialism, exclusion, purity, and dietary laws.

When Jesus did quote Leviticus, He emphasized the positive mandate to "love your neighbor as yourself" (Leviticus 19:18, NIV), ignoring the negative mandates.

Jesus possessed a discerning insight, recognizing which passages aligned with God's true intentions and which were mere cultural, self-serving, or legalistic additions. When Christians insist that every line in the Bible holds equal importance or authority, they diverge from Jesus's approach. Let us never forget that the Bible is a means to an end, not the end itself. Our ultimate aim is to know and follow Jesus Christ, the embodiment of God's Word. The Bible serves as a roadmap, guiding us toward Him. Our interpretations and applications of Scripture should always be rooted in His teachings of love, compassion, and mercy.

CHAPTER 4

WHATEVER HAPPENED TO THE TRINITY?

In the beginning was the relationship.
To speak the name of Jesus Christ biblically, in the tradition of the apostles and the early Church, is to say, "Father's eternal Son," and it is to say, "the One anointed in the Holy Spirit," and it is to say, "the Creator and Sustainer of all things—incarnate, crucified, resurrected, and ascended." Thus, to speak the name of Jesus Christ is to say, "The blessed Trinity, and fallen humanity, and broken creation, are not separated but together in relationship." Jesus is himself the relationship.[14]

Perichoresis is a concept describing the dynamic relationship among the three persons of the triune God—Father, Son, and Holy Spirit. The early church fathers coined perichoresis to represent their endeavor to comprehend and engage with the mystery of the Trinity. It portrays the relational dynamics and vitality inherent in the inter-theistic unity of the Godhead. The imagery of God in a dance, perpetually extending an invitation for us

---
14 Barth, Karl. *Church Dogmatics*. Edited by G. W. Bromiley and T. F. Torrance. Translated by G. T. Thomson and Harold Knight. Vol. 1, *The Doctrine of the Word of God: Prolegomena to Church Dogmatics*. Edinburgh: T. & T. Clark, 1956.

to join in—the dance of relationship—is a central motif in the understanding of perichoresis by the early church fathers.

The significance of the doctrine of the Trinity lies in its foundation of goodness and love. If we envision a solitary deity throughout eternity, it inevitably leads to a conception of God as isolated and self-centered, lacking relational depth. Such a deity would be unapproachable, impersonal, and devoid of goodness, as goodness inherently involves relational dynamics. Furthermore, genuine love necessitates an object to be loved, and in the absence of another, love would devolve into self-centeredness, far removed from the selfless love that agape epitomizes.

THE TRINITY ASSERTS THAT AT THE CORE OF GOD'S ETERNAL EXISTENCE LIES FELLOWSHIP, OTHER-CENTEREDNESS, AND APPROACHABILITY—THE ESSENCE OF COMMUNION CHARACTERIZED BY SELF-GIVING AND SACRIFICE IN RELATIONSHIP TO THE OTHER.

This is where the doctrine of the Trinity becomes indispensable. It asserts that at the core of God's eternal existence lies fellowship, other-centeredness, and approachability—the essence of communion characterized by self-giving and sacrifice in relationship to the other. Thus, the Trinity grounds the very essence of God's being in a relational context, highlighting His eternal self-giving nature and underscoring the importance of communion and sacrificial love in the divine nature.

The foundation of trust lies in understanding that we can place our trust in the Father, Son, and Spirit because their eternal relationship sets the standard for how they interact. Their unwavering trust and love for one another throughout eternity serve as the blueprint for how they relate to us. If there were doubts between them—perhaps the Holy Spirit questioning the Father's heart or the Father questioning Jesus or the Holy Spirit—it would give us cause for hesitation in trusting them. However, when we witness in the New Testament the profound love between the Father, Son, and Spirit—how the Father loves the Son, as Jesus demonstrates through His actions, and how the Son aligns Himself completely with the Father's will—it reveals a relationship of beauty and goodness that is entirely focused on others. This is the same way they relate to each of us.

Now, we have a foundation rooted in the essence of God, assuring us of His trustworthiness, goodness, and justice toward us. The God who encompasses all is inherently good—Athanasius described Him as "supremely noble by nature," reflecting the intrinsic character of God. It's crucial to note that when Athanasius speaks of this noble nature, he's not referring to a solitary individual but to the Trinity itself. Thus, by His very nature, God encompasses all that is inherently good and supremely noble.

Consequently, this God is the ultimate lover of humanity. Trust can only truly emerge from this understanding. When doubt seeps into our perception of God—which often happens in various ways within Christian communities and our approach to the gospel—our ability to trust in Him becomes compromised.

Yet, we can find confidence in the fact that God's trustworthiness confirms His desire for us.

> "When Christ who is your life appears, then you also will appear with him in glory." —Colossians 3:4

Our existence finds its true significance within the framework of relationships. Typically, individuals who exhibit toxic, psychopathic, or sociopathic tendencies struggle to maintain meaningful connections and often shy away from or sabotage relationships, leading to a solitary existence or making interactions with them challenging. Loneliness often lies at the root of many mental health issues, and disconnection stands as a significant cause of distress and suffering for humanity.

When we isolate ourselves from others, we risk falling into a state of sickness and toxicity, straying from the path of godliness. The depth of relational connectedness goes beyond our comprehension, which is why God places such paramount importance on relationships. Perichoresis encapsulates the divine dance within the Godhead—an intricately balanced and profoundly intimate relationship that embodies vulnerability and harmony.

As we delve deeper into contemplating our connection with the divine Trinity, it's essential to consider the profound significance of the incarnation—the embodiment of God in human form, as Jesus. The early church staunchly defended the doctrine of the incarnation because they recognized its pivotal importance. They understood that everything hinged upon this truth.

If Jesus is not fully divine, then what He offers us falls short of the fullness and life of God. Conversely, if Jesus is not fully human, although divine, He fails to fully relate to us. Without this complete humanity, His reach toward humanity remains incomplete, leaving us ultimately separated from Him. Consequently, we would only be able to observe the intimate relationship within the Trinity from a distance.

IF JESUS IS NOT FULLY DIVINE, THEN WHAT HE OFFERS US FALLS SHORT OF THE FULLNESS AND LIFE OF GOD. CONVERSELY, IF JESUS IS NOT FULLY HUMAN, ALTHOUGH DIVINE, HE FAILS TO FULLY RELATE TO US.

While the significance of both the divinity and humanity of Jesus cannot be overstated, it's crucial to also emphasize a third aspect of the incarnation that is equally vital. Through the incarnation, God not only took on human form but became a genuine human being—sharing in our humanity, bone of our bone, and flesh of our flesh. This was not just any deity; this was the Son of God, the beloved Son—not some distant, nebulous entity floating in outer space. This is the beloved Son who dwells in intimate fellowship with the Father through the Spirit, the One who intimately knows and loves the Father and partakes in the divine dance of life.

Above and beyond all things, the incarnation means the coming not merely of God or some kind of generic divine life. The incarnation means the coming of the eternal trinitarian relationship of Father, Son and Spirit.

> *In Jesus Christ, not just divine life, but the great dance of the Trinity, the joy and fullness and glory of the Father, Son and Spirit, their life and communion and fellowship, entered into our world and set up shop. That is the simple and astonishing truth of it.*[15]

> *"For in him all the fullness of God was pleased to dwell."—Colossians 1:19*

> *"For in him the whole fullness of deity dwells bodily."—Colossians 2:9*

The life of Jesus embodies not only divine existence but also the very essence of Trinitarian life within human experience. Through the incarnation of Jesus, the sublime dance of the Trinity becomes tangible and finds expression in human form, intertwining divine and human realities into a harmonious whole. When Jesus took on human form, it wasn't a temporary guise. His embodiment of humanity wasn't just for a limited time, only to be discarded afterward. Jesus permanently united Himself with humanity, becoming one of us—sharing in our humanity completely, as bone of our bone and flesh of our flesh. His earthly experience wasn't merely a transient episode in God's eternal life; rather, it became an enduring reality for the Trinity.

Even now, Jesus is seated at the right hand of the Father in heavenly realms, participating in the divine dance as both fully God and fully man. Before the incarnation, the Trinity existed

---

[15] This lecture was originally delivered at The Institute for the Study of Trinitarian Theology, Jackson, MS as part of the first series of lectures entitled "The Big Picture: From the Trinity to Our Adoption in Christ."

as a divine dance, but through the incarnation, the triune life became a divine-human dance. This profound union represents the ultimate and most intimate expression of the divine reaching out to humanity—and reach us it did.

The incarnation represents Jesus, the beloved Son, fully embracing His sonship and intimate fellowship with the Father while existing as a human being. Jesus didn't merely manifest His divinity within human existence; rather, He embodied divinity within human "flesh." The creation of the heavens and the earth wasn't solely the work of God in a generic sense, but rather the Father, Son, and Holy Spirit actively involved in the process of creation.

> "And the Word became flesh and dwelt among us, and we have seen his glory, glory as of the only Son from the Father, full of grace and truth."—John 1:14

Here we stand in awe before the exquisite mystery of the very essence of God. Three divine persons intricately intertwined within each other in indivisible unity yet retaining their distinct personhood—this is *perichoresis*. There exists no dimension of divine being deeper than or beyond the communion of the blessed Three, who eternally dwell in indivisible oneness and boundless love. This relationship between Father, Son, and Spirit is not a recent development or a mere guise assumed during the incarnation; it predates Christmas morning. It is the eternal essence of God, unchanging throughout time and eternity. This divine relationship serves as the creative womb from which all creation emerges.

> "Before long, the world will not see me anymore, but you will see me. Because I live, you also will live. On that day you will realize that I am in my Father, and you are in me, and I am in you."—John 14:19-20 (NIV)

A RICH TRINITARIAN HISTORY

The roots of the doctrine of the Trinity can be traced back to the pages of the New Testament, where glimpses of this complex unity between Father, Son, and Holy Spirit are scattered throughout the writings of the apostles. While the term "Trinity" itself does not appear in the Bible, the foundational principles underlying the doctrine emerge from passages such as the baptismal formula in Matthew 28:19, "Baptizing them in the name of the Father and of the Son and of the Holy Spirit" and the apostolic benedictions invoking the grace of the Lord Jesus Christ, the love of God, and the fellowship of the Holy Spirit (see 2 Corinthians 13:14).

In the early centuries of Christianity, attempts to articulate the nature of God and the relationship between the Father, Son, and Holy Spirit led to the formulation of various theological expressions. The writings of the apostolic fathers, such as Ignatius of Antioch and Clement of Rome, laid the groundwork for the development of Trinitarian thought, emphasizing the unity of God while acknowledging the distinct roles of the three divine persons.

The first major challenge to the emerging doctrine of the Trinity came in the form of Arianism, a theological movement the presbyter Arius led in the fourth century. Arius's teachings, which emphasized the subordination of the Son to the Father and denied the co-eternity and co-equality of the divine persons, sparked fierce debates within the early Christian community.

In response to the Arian controversy, Emperor Constantine convened the First Council of Nicaea in 325 AD, bringing together bishops from across the Christian world to address the doctrinal disputes. At Nicaea, the assembled bishops affirmed the divinity of Christ in opposition to Arianism and formulated the Nicene Creed, which articulated the orthodox belief in the consubstantiality of the Son with the Father.

Despite the efforts of the Nicene Council, theological debates surrounding the Trinity continued to simmer in the centuries that followed. The controversy resurfaced with renewed intensity in the fifth century, culminating in the Council of Chalcedon in 451 AD, which addressed questions related to the nature of Christ's personhood and affirmed the orthodox understanding of the Trinity.

In the wake of the early ecumenical councils, the doctrine of the Trinity gradually became more firmly established within the theological framework of Christianity. The works of theologians such as Augustine of Hippo in the West and the Cappadocian Fathers—Basil the Great, Gregory of Nyssa, and Gregory of Nazianzus—in the East played a pivotal role in elucidating the mysteries of the Trinity and articulating its implications for Christian life and worship.

Throughout the medieval period, theologians continued to explore the intricacies of Trinitarian theology, drawing upon the rich theological heritage of the early church fathers and engaging with philosophical currents of their time. The doctrine of the Trinity remained a central focus of theological reflection, shaping the theological landscape of the medieval scholastic period and beyond.

The Protestant Reformation of the sixteenth century brought new perspectives and challenges to the doctrine of the Trinity, as reformers sought to return to the sources of Christian faith and grappled with questions of authority and interpretation. While the Reformers affirmed the foundational tenets of Trinitarian belief, theological differences emerged within Protestant traditions regarding the understanding of divine sovereignty, human freedom, and the role of the Spirit in the Christian life.

THE DOCTRINE OF THE TRINITY CONTINUES TO INSPIRE THEOLOGICAL REFLECTION AND SPIRITUAL DEVOTION, SERVING AS A PROFOUND EXPRESSION OF THE MYSTERY AND MAJESTY OF GOD'S TRIUNE NATURE.

In the modern era, advances in biblical scholarship, historical research, and interfaith dialogue have further enriched the study of the Trinity, fostering greater theological dialogue and ecumenical cooperation among Christians of diverse traditions. The doctrine of the Trinity continues to inspire theological reflection and spiritual devotion, serving as a profound expression of the mystery and majesty of God's triune nature.

The history of the doctrine of the Trinity is a testament to the enduring quest of Christian theologians and thinkers to apprehend the divine mystery of God's triune nature. From the theological debates of the early church to the challenges and controversies of subsequent centuries, the doctrine of the Trinity has served as a touchstone of Christian orthodoxy and a source of profound spiritual insight.

Amidst the rich tapestry of history, it appeared that the emphasis on the Trinity had largely faded within the modern Western church. While discussions surrounding the Trinity often resonated more with Eastern spiritual approaches, there seemed to be a noticeable absence of genuine focus on the Trinity for a significant period. Gratefully, individuals like Baxter Kruger, Paul Young, and Richard Rohr, among others, emerged as voices who penned profoundly beautiful and awe-inspiring works, reigniting a revival of Trinitarianism once more.

Paul Young's book likely had the most widespread impact on the Western church's renewed attention to the Trinity. *The Shack* is a novel that tells the story of Mackenzie "Mack" Phillips, a man struggling with immense grief and anger following the abduction and presumed murder of his youngest daughter. One winter day, Mack receives a mysterious note inviting him to return to the shack in the Oregon wilderness, where evidence of his daughter's murder is found. Reluctantly, Mack ventures to the shack, where he encounters manifestations of the Holy Trinity—God the Father portrayed as an African-American woman named Papa, Jesus as a Middle Eastern man named Sarayu, and the Holy Spirit as an Asian woman named Elousia. Through conversations and experiences with these representations of the Trinity, Mack confronts his pain, wrestles with questions of faith and forgiveness, and ultimately finds healing and reconciliation.[16]

---

[16] William P. Young, *The Shack: Where Tragedy Confronts Eternity* (Thousand Oaks, CA: Windblown Media, July 1, 2007).

Whether or not you enjoyed reading *The Shack*, it undeniably prompted conversations about the Trinity. And sometimes, that's all it takes to spark progress. Silence rarely leads to movement, but discussion opens doors to new and insightful inquiries. Thought-provoking questions often pave the way for exciting discoveries.

THE REAL (MYSTICAL) GENESIS

In the introductory section of this book, I highlighted various fields of study that ultimately left me wanting. It's important to clarify that this isn't a criticism of the individuals who pioneered these areas of inquiry. In fact, much of what I explored served as essential building blocks that have led me to my current understanding. To me, this serves as yet another testament to the graciousness of God's presence on our journey. God accompanies us as we navigate through our pursuits and interpretations of Him, even when our assertions about Him range from naive to downright distressing. Despite our shortcomings, He remains patient with us, guiding us along the path from confusion to enlightenment, much like He did with the figures of faith throughout Scripture.

Throughout my years of study, one glaring omission for me was the absence of a robust or sometimes even existing exploration of Trinitarian theology. While I was introduced to the concept of the Trinity in Bible school, there was a noticeable lack of discussion on how this profound doctrine could influence my daily relationship with God, shape my interpretation of Scripture, or even transform my perspective on life itself. Somehow, along the journey, the significance of the Trinity seemed to fade into the background. I inadvertently compartmentalized something that can never truly be separated.

WAS IT POSSIBLE TO RECONCILE THE CONFLICTING IMAGES OF GOD WITH THE GOD I INTIMATELY KNEW AND LOVED?

As I reflected on my journey, I yearned for a fresh start. I continually encountered obstacles in my quest to grasp the authentic nature of God. Was He akin to Janus, the two-faced Roman god, oscillating between vengeance and mercy? Was He genuinely other-centered, or did He demand numerous sacrifices to appease His wrath? Why did I find it effortless to love Jesus, while thoughts of the Father, particularly in the Old Testament, stirred feelings of fear and distrust? Could there be a reset capable of fulfilling the deep longing in my heart? Was it possible to reconcile the conflicting images of God with the God I intimately knew and loved? Thankfully, the solution had been right in front of me all along—a grand reset or "re-genesis," if you will. Despite lacking a better term, the moment to truly perceive it had finally arrived.

In the beginning was the Word, and the Word was with God, and the Word was God. He was in the beginning with God. All things were made through Him, and without Him nothing was made that was made. In Him was life, and the life was the light of men. And the light shines in the darkness, and the darkness did not comprehend it. And the Word became flesh and dwelt among us, and we beheld His glory, the glory as of the only begotten of the Father, full of grace and truth. —John 1:1-5, 14 (NKJV)

The re-genesis I had been seeking was right before my eyes all along! The genesis described in John 1 predates the events narrated in the opening chapters of the book of Genesis. The Word referenced in John 1 encapsulates the very essence of God, and when that Word takes on human form, we recognize Him as Jesus. This re-genesis, this cosmic anthropology through which we all find placement, isn't merely a collection of sixty-six books neatly bound in leather; rather, it embodies the living, creative, and transformative essence that is the all-loving, authentic, and clear relational Godhead.

The profound truth of the unified Godhead has remained constant throughout history. Regardless of where we encounter un-Christlike depictions, even within the Scriptures themselves, Jesus serves as the perfect lens through which we understand these images. Similarly, regardless of the legalistic transactions or covenant frameworks we may impose on our relationship with God, Jesus provides the ultimate interpretation of these experiences. No veil placed on God, as referenced in 2 Corinthians 3:13-18, could ever alter His character and nature. Instead, such veils merely acted as blank slates onto which we projected our own interpretations, akin to Rorschach images.

The Father is unmistakably revealed in the person of Jesus Christ. Jesus Himself declared, "If you have seen Me, you have seen the Father" (John 14:9, author paraphrase). The book of Hebrews affirms, "God, after He spoke long ago to the fathers in the prophets in many portions and in many ways, in these last days has spoken to us in His Son" (Hebrews 1:1-2, NASB). Moreover, Jesus is described as "the exact representation of His nature." God's primary communication is now through the person and actions of Jesus. The two are perfectly alike.

"Long ago, at many times and in many ways, God spoke to our fathers by the prophets, but in these last days he has spoken to us by his Son, whom he appointed the heir of all things, through whom also he created the world."—Hebrews 1:1-2

Jesus perfectly illuminates the portrayals of God in the old covenant and epitomizes the pure revelation of the God depicted in the old covenant. It's intriguing how much of our obscured perception of God tends to create a false dichotomy between Jesus and our loving Father. If Jesus healed all who approached Him, yet the Father supposedly wills sickness upon people, it suggests a fractured unity within *perichoresis*. Jesus calmed storms and brought peace (see Mark 4:35-41); He didn't unleash natural disasters as a form of judgment upon specific groups of people. To truly comprehend God, one must look to Jesus for understanding. He has completely removed the veil, once and for all.

WHEN WE GRASP THE ESSENCE OF GOD, WE REALIZE THAT JESUS ISN'T IN CONFLICT WITH THE FATHER TO UNVEIL A NEW STANDARD; RATHER, HE FLAWLESSLY MIRRORS AND EMBODIES THE FATHER'S NATURE.

When we grasp the essence of God, we realize that Jesus isn't in conflict with the Father to unveil a new standard; rather, He flawlessly mirrors and embodies the Father's nature. This understanding is crucial, especially since many hold the belief that Jesus ultimately intervenes on our behalf to shield us from the destruction and calamity supposedly willed by God. The perception of a compassionate Jesus standing between us and an indifferent God has permeated the church for quite some time. Is it any surprise that the world shares this perspective? After all, they've inherited their theology from us!

I find it intriguing that we tend to favor the literal creation narrative as the starting point in our Bibles, considering that the majority of the content focuses on humanity—our sins, misunderstandings, wars, and challenges. Essentially, the narrative revolves around us, with God occasionally woven into the fabric. When we anchor our beginning with the book of Genesis, it becomes apparent how our self-projections about God take center stage in the Old Testament narrative. Fortunately, the genuine genesis described in John 1 not only affirms the truth of the mystical union within the Godhead but also offers a lens through which we can reevaluate everything.

It would be greatly beneficial to maintain a focus on the Trinity throughout the remainder of this book. This perspective offers numerous advantages, but perhaps most significantly, it underscores the profound truth that the Godhead cannot be fragmented. For instance, when we encounter instances like God purportedly opening the earth and swallowing Korah, Dathan, Abiram, and their families whole because they claimed equality with Moses and Aaron, we can analyze such events through the lens of Jesus. Or when God vows not to let mercy or compassion deter Him from shattering families even though He commands their wholesale slaughter (see Jeremiah 13:14). In such passages, I propose that we are witnessing a reflection of the flawed, fallen, and culturally conditioned perception of God that Jeremiah and other ancient Israelites held. As the perfect representation of the Father, Jesus reveals that such behavior is not consistent with the character of God, despite being attributed to Him.

In upcoming chapters, we will delve into overarching themes concerning un-Christlike depictions of God. However, it's crucial to reiterate a simple rule of thumb for now. If any belief about God fails to resemble Jesus, there is a gap in understanding. Likewise, if any image of God does not mirror the exact likeness of Jesus, it warrants questioning. Should any discrepancy arise among the Blessed Three, all imagery must yield to Jesus. Such is the intimacy of their relationship! There exists no Father apart from the Son, nor Son apart from the Holy Spirit. The Three are indivisible, perfectly related in union.

IF ANY BELIEF ABOUT GOD FAILS TO RESEMBLE JESUS, THERE IS A GAP IN UNDERSTANDING.

"O mystic marvel! The universal Father is one, and one the universal Word; and the Holy Spirit is one and the same everywhere...."
—Clement of Alexandria, The Instructor[17]

---

[17] The Paedagogus (Book I)-Clement of Alexandria.

CHAPTER 5

THE SERMON ON THE MOUNT: THE JESUS (GODHEAD) WAY

"Jesus's first miracle was [turning] water into wine because He knew you needed a stiff drink before He obliterated everything you knew about God."
—John Crowder

The Sermon on the Mount stands as arguably the most profound sermon ever delivered. It serves as a stark contrast to the previous system established before Jesus, which relied on laws, works, and the Mosaic covenant. Instead, Jesus introduces a new paradigm—a better covenant founded on righteousness. Beyond eloquent rhetoric, the Sermon on the Mount lays a robust foundation for life in the kingdom. Jesus doesn't construct this foundation with a set of new rules; rather, He reveals the exquisite nuances of God's character and nature through real-life situations. This is why all who heard His words were astonished, and why they continue to challenge and amaze us today.

The Sermon on the Mount bore little resemblance to the modern "lectern ministry" prevalent in much of the Western church today. Interestingly, Jesus didn't even command anyone to listen to His words, nor did He vie for attention. His focus was solely on those with whom He had significant relational bonds. While others were welcome to stay and receive, Jesus ensured that His disciples would grasp the radical truths He was about to impart. The crowd's lingering presence can be attributed to two factors: the revolutionary content of His message and the undeniable authority with which He spoke.

Jesus spoke with an authority, unlike anything that had been heard before. Even now, when we encounter His words from the Sermon on the Mount, we sense the power and conviction with which Christ spoke—not only to His immediate audience but also to generations that would follow. His words resonate with timeless wisdom, comforting our hearts and inspiring us to live as imitators of our good Father. Christ Himself lived in obedience to the Father, seeking to bring Him glory and to reveal His authentic character and nature. Similarly, we are designed and destined to do likewise.

Jesus was always intentional in His actions and words. Just as Exodus 19:3 describes how God called Moses from the mountain to deliver His message, some scholars suggest that Jesus deliberately chose a mountainside for His teachings. In Matthew 5, Jesus challenges established Scripture and traditions six times with the authoritative declaration, "But I say to you" (see Matthew 5:22, 28, 32, 39, 44). The primary aim of the Sermon on the Mount was to cast light on the shadows of the old law, revealing its true meaning within the context of the new covenant. Through this teaching, the traditional perceptions of God, which had been shaped over time, underwent radical redefinition in light of the revelation of Jesus.

In Matthew 5:17, Jesus declares, "Do not think that I have come to abolish the Law or the Prophets; I have not come to abolish them but to fulfill them."

WE ARE CALLED TO SUBMIT THE AUTHORITY OF OUR LIVES TO CHRIST, ALLOWING HIS GOODNESS AND LOVE TO FLOW THROUGH US.

During Jesus's time, the Old Testament Scriptures held a certain glory, yet they didn't fully reveal the authentic heart and nature of God embodied in Jesus Himself. The people of that era struggled to grasp the entirety of Jesus's message because they were entrenched in religious traditions and rules that seemed to define their worthiness before God. Jesus, however, brought something revolutionary—an expansion and fulfillment of the divine narrative that may have seemed too good to be true to those steeped in legalism. Today, the timeless relevance of Jesus's words echoes through the ages. We are called to submit the authority of our lives to Christ, allowing His goodness and love to flow through us. In embracing Christ, we are transformed into new creations, reflecting His character and embodying His teachings in our lives.

In a pivotal moment at the start of the Sermon on the Mount, Jesus challenges our perceptions of God's nature. He reveals God's true image in Matthew 5:43-45 (NKJV), saying:

"You have heard that it was said, 'You shall love your neighbor and hate your enemy.' But I tell you, love your enemies, bless those who curse you, do good to those who hate you, and pray for those who spitefully use you and persecute you, that you may be sons of your Father in heaven."

The world often operates on a principle of retaliation: "an eye for an eye, a tooth for a tooth." Initially, this may seem like a justified response when we feel wronged. However, Jesus advocates for a different approach to everyday conflicts in challenge of this mindset. He urges us to "turn the other cheek," "go the extra mile," and be generous to those in need. Jesus isn't just presenting humanity with a better way of living; He's also unveiling the timeless ways of the Godhead that were previously hidden.

The concept of "an eye for an eye" was originally instituted in Mosaic law to prevent personal acts of revenge. It allowed individuals to seek justice through the governing judicial system rather than taking matters into their own hands. This principle ensured that punishments fit the crimes, deterring future wrongdoing. However, this law is often misunderstood and misapplied, leading to justification for personal revenge. Instead of promoting justice, it becomes a tool for retaliation. To address this misconception, Jesus encourages a response rooted in love and forgiveness rather than retaliation and revenge. He challenges us to break free from the cycle of retaliation and embrace a mindset of compassion and grace.

Those hearing the words of Matthew 5:43-45 understood they served as a radical re-imaging of the character and nature of God. Let's see how.

POINT ONE: DOES GOD HATE PEOPLE?

It appears that the Bible mentions instances where God is described as hating certain individuals. For example, Romans 9:13 indicates that God hated Esau even before his birth due to Esau inheriting Adam's disdain for God, and God chose not to elect Esau for salvation. Similarly, Psalm 5:5 (NIV) states, "The arrogant cannot stand in Your presence; You hate all who do wrong," illustrating that God's hatred is directed towards individuals rather than abstract concepts of sin or wickedness. Psalm 139:21-22 urges us to align ourselves with God's righteous indignation towards those who oppose Him: "Do I not hate those who hate You, LORD? . . . I have nothing but hatred for them; I count them my enemies" (NIV). Similarly, Revelation 2:6 echoes this sentiment in the New Testament.

How should we interpret this? One suggestion is that in certain instances, "hate" may simply imply "love to a lesser extent." For instance, in Luke 14:26, Jesus instructs us to prioritize Him over even our own family members, while in the corresponding passage in Matthew 10:37, He emphasizes loving Him more than our family. While this explanation may alleviate some of the tension surrounding the concept of hate, does it truly provide clarity regarding the nature of the God revealed in Jesus? However, this interpretation doesn't suffice for the verses mentioned earlier. God didn't love Esau less than Jacob; rather, He didn't extend any saving love to Esau at all.

Psalm 139:21-22 appears to offer some additional perspective on the "hate" issue. Hatred, as portrayed in the Bible, is not primarily an emotion but a covenant action. It signifies counting someone as an enemy and treating them as such. When God is said to hate someone, it means He has chosen not to favor them, leading to their eventual destruction. In essence, there are both "soft" and "hard" senses of hatred. When God loves someone, He chooses to favor them; when He hates someone, He chooses not to favor them. Therefore, we are called to prioritize Christ over our own family members, just as God favored Jacob over Esau. We are to align ourselves with God's friends and refrain from favoring His enemies, as depicted in Psalm 139.

Does this explanation of hatred sufficiently soften the apparent contradiction, allowing us to conclude that Jesus has provided clarity regarding a God who seemingly harbors hatred and disfavor toward others? The referenced verses indeed seem to suggest that we are permitted to hate and withhold favor from those whom God similarly hates and does not favor. However, does it seem that Jesus endorses such behavior, especially in light of His unwavering commandment to love our enemies and to do good to those who hate us? I would argue that the love Jesus commands us to extend to those who hate us directly opposes the language of "hate" found elsewhere in Scripture. This is just one instance demonstrating how Jesus resolves apparent contradictions within the Bible as well as illuminates our projected shadow images of God.

I WOULD ARGUE THAT THE LOVE JESUS COMMANDS US TO EXTEND TO THOSE WHO HATE US DIRECTLY OPPOSES THE LANGUAGE OF "HATE" FOUND ELSEWHERE IN SCRIPTURE.

The most profound example of divine love is detailed in 1 John 4. The same John, who introduces us to the cosmic Christ at the beginning of his Gospel and provides a breathtaking glimpse of the unveiling of Jesus Christ in Revelation through beautiful apocalyptic imagery, delves deeply into the concept of agape. He emphasizes that love isn't merely a choice that God makes but rather that love is inherent to God's nature. In other words, "Love is the essence of God." This revelation of divine agape appears to directly contradict the notion of a God who hates His beloved creation or would ever encourage us to hate others.

POINT TWO: DOES GOD APPROVE OF RETALIATION?

In Leviticus 24:19-22, we encounter the establishment of the law of retaliation within the nation of Israel attributed directly to God. It stipulates that if a person causes injury to their neighbor, the same injury shall be inflicted upon them: "fracture for fracture, eye for eye, tooth for tooth." Furthermore, the law mandates that if someone kills an animal, they must make restitution, but if they kill a person, they will face capital punishment. This law applies equally to both strangers and native citizens, emphasizing the divine authority behind it: "I am the LORD your God."

Now, consider the legal system attributed to God that the Israelites adhered to for generations. Then, envision Jesus, the perfect representation of God, who completely challenges and overturns this system. As a member of the inseparable Trinity, Jesus offers us profound insight into the true nature of His Father. So, who truly embodies the heart of God? Is it the Israelites with their "eye for an eye" retaliation system, or is it Jesus, who instructs us to do good, bless, and pray for those who persecute us? When Jesus, the Son within the Trinity, presents an image of His Father that contradicts other texts about Him, it's wise to align with Jesus.

Let me be clear that God wants us to take actions of personal revenge out of our hands. In modern scenarios, we can turn offenders over to the governmental authorities if appropriate, and even if that doesn't work, we should always desire to turn them over to the trustworthy hands of God Himself. As Paul states in Romans: "Repay no one evil for evil. . . . Beloved, do not avenge yourselves, but *rather* give place to wrath; for it is written 'Vengeance is Mine, I will repay,' says the Lord" (Romans 12:17, 19, NKJV). We can now quote the above verse with confidence when we understand the revelation of God reflected through the crucified Christ, as one who does not dole out "vengeance" as a punitive judge but as a restorative Father.

THE BEATITUDES: THE CHARACTER OF THE GODHEAD

As we explore the Beatitudes, it's important to frame our discussion in terms of the kingdom. The kingdom of God can be understood in various ways, but in this context, it refers to the internal sovereignty and influence of the character and essence of the Divine Trinity. Simply put, the kingdom isn't primarily a physical location or a governmental system, but rather the expression of a Person—Jesus.

In each of Jesus's Beatitudes, He reveals the profound truth that the kingdom of heaven is accessible now, especially to those who consider themselves unworthy. They also highlight a stark contrast for those who believe they are deserving but are not.

Take the first beatitude, for instance. Jesus graciously declares that the kingdom belongs to those who acknowledge their spiritual poverty. Yet, He also admonishes the religious elite who boast in their achievements. Indeed, the spiritually affluent must humble themselves before God to realize that their accomplishments do not grant them entry into the kingdom of God.

> **SIMPLY PUT, THE KINGDOM ISN'T PRIMARILY A PHYSICAL LOCATION OR A GOVERNMENTAL SYSTEM, BUT RATHER THE EXPRESSION OF A PERSON—JESUS.**

The Beatitudes hold significant teaching for Jesus's followers. The virtues that characterized the righteous person in the Old Testament now become a lived reality with the advent of God's kingdom. These virtues accompany the change that takes place in the life of every disciple as they yield to the influence of kingdom life through the Spirit. In the Beatitudes, and throughout the Sermon on the Mount, the focus is on a righteousness that starts with inner transformation and then extends to align external actions with internal principles.

The issue with the scribes and Pharisees lay in their emphasis on outward righteousness. Jesus, however, shifts the focus to the inner transformation of the heart through the advent of the kingdom of heaven. This transformation encompasses every aspect of the individual—speech, thoughts, actions, and behavior. While this alignment between inner and outer life was always

God's intent since creation, it is now actualized with the arrival of the kingdom of heaven through Jesus's ministry. The Beatitudes serve as declarations of the character qualities that will naturally emerge in disciples who engage in kingdom living.

The Beatitudes aren't commands or strict standards that disciples must follow to earn God's approval. If they were, they'd resemble the strict purity demands of the Jewish leaders, leading to the hypocrisy Jesus condemns. Instead, they outline the kind of life God desires to cultivate in His disciples. As the kingdom of God takes root in each disciple, these character traits become tangible realities. This connection between Jesus's teachings on discipleship and later New Testament discussions on Holy Spirit regeneration and sanctification is evident. For instance, Peter describes this transformative process in those born anew by God's enduring Word, echoing the imagery of the incarnate Word declared in John 1 (see 1 Peter 1:22–2:3). Facing daily challenges in a fallen world, disciples must allow God's Spirit to nurture these Christlike qualities within them.

As we explore the Beatitudes, let's consider them not only as qualities for us to strive to exhibit and show the world but also as attributes of the unchanging Godhead. This perspective profoundly influences our comprehension of God's character and nature, shedding light on the "Rorschach Imagery" found in other scripturally informed images that appear un-Christlike.

As we explore each Beatitude and invoke the name of Jesus or God or Holy Spirit, let's imagine not only the embodied God (Jesus) but also recognize that this representation encompasses the entirety of the Godhead (Father, Son, Holy Spirit). In the interconnected relationship of the Trinity, there is no division or gap. Thus, these standards of character cannot be exclusive to Jesus alone; rather, He illuminates the timeless character and essence of the entire Godhead.

Beatitude One: Blessed Are the Poor

The term "poor" refers not only to those facing economic hardship but also to individuals who are spiritually and emotionally burdened, disheartened, and in need of divine assistance. This initial beatitude challenges the common belief that material prosperity signifies God's favor and automatically accompanies spiritual well-being. Rather, Jesus emphasizes that in the kingdom of heaven, the standard is spiritual emptiness (humility, spiritual poverty), contrasting with the spiritual self-reliance often seen in religious leaders.

In Philippians 2:5-8, we learn that Jesus not only understands what it means to be poor in spirit but also embodies this state. These verses reveal:

Have this attitude in yourselves which was also in Christ Jesus, who, as He already existed in the form of God, did not consider equality with God something to be grasped, but emptied Himself by taking the form of a bond-servant and *being born in the likeness of men. And being found in appearance as a man, He humbled Himself by becoming obedient to the point of death: death on a cross. (NASB)*

When we contemplate the first beatitude, we see that the divine Godhead has consistently embodied authentic humility. Recognizing this truth enables us to embrace spiritual poverty with genuine joy and trust since we do not need to rely on ourselves.

Beatitude Two: Blessed Are Those Who Mourn

Experiencing the loss of anything deemed valuable inevitably leads to mourning, whether it's financial security, loved ones, societal status, or even spiritual grief. However, mourning doesn't negate the joy characteristic of Jesus's followers; instead, it amplifies the resilience and strength that joy brings into our lives. While suffering is an inevitable aspect of human existence, the life imparted to us through Jesus ensures that our suffering is never the final destination but a pathway to something greater.

"Jesus wept" (John 11:35) stands out as one of the simplest yet most profoundly moving verses in the Bible. The term "wept" here doesn't denote intense wailing but rather a serene shedding of tears. With full awareness of the impending resurrection of Lazarus, Jesus compassionately shared in the grief of Mary, Martha, and their loved ones. He didn't hastily move past their emotions, offering a quick fix. Instead, this moment beautifully demonstrates the perfect harmony between his humanity and divinity.

When seeking to understand human grief, we can find no greater example than the experience of the Son of God Himself, as described in Isaiah 53:3 as "a man of sorrows, and acquainted with grief." This highlights a fundamental aspect of human existence following the long-experienced delusion man believed of there being distance and separation between ourselves and the Godhead: our acquaintance with grief.

In Christ, our grief is transient. Despite our sorrows, we cling to hope in God's fulfilled redemption and triumph, mirroring Jesus's stance. He mourned, knowing a time would come when all tears would cease. Our hope in God's steadfast goodness navigates us through grief, fostering our profound connection with Him and humanity. It's in this journey where we discover solace, happiness, and communion with fellow believers. Therefore, grief becomes a testament of faith as we journey through life.

"Blessed be the God and Father of our Lord Jesus Christ, the Father of mercies and God of all comfort, who comforts us in all our affliction, so that we will be able to comfort those who are in any affliction with the comfort with which we ourselves are comforted by God."—2 Corinthians 1:3-4 (NASB)

As we contemplate the second beatitude, it's clear that the divine Godhead is not merely a witness to our mourning but is an active participant. We do not have to mourn alone, nor do we mourn without hope. It's appropriate for us to sit, weep, and empathize with the pain and suffering of others. Engaging in such a privilege is profoundly sacred, embodying selfless faith.

Beatitude Three: Blessed Are the Meek

Those who seek to dominate and assert themselves often strive to establish their own kingdoms on earth. However, Jesus teaches that it is the "gentle" who will ultimately inherit the earth, echoing the sentiments of the psalmist who comforts those whom wrongdoers mistreat. Jesus Himself exemplifies true gentleness. It requires great strength to align others with God's will, but when that strength is paired with humble non-aggression, it yields a gentle individual capable of enduring trials patiently to fulfill God's plans for His people.

> **IT REQUIRES GREAT STRENGTH TO ALIGN OTHERS WITH GOD'S WILL, BUT WHEN THAT STRENGTH IS PAIRED WITH HUMBLE NON-AGGRESSION, IT YIELDS A GENTLE INDIVIDUAL CAPABLE OF ENDURING TRIALS PATIENTLY TO FULFILL GOD'S PLANS FOR HIS PEOPLE.**

"From the days of John the Baptist until now the kingdom of heaven has suffered violence, and the violent take it by force."—Matthew 11:12

Meekness appears contrary to the portrayals of God in the Old Testament, where He is often depicted as commanding acts of violence against nations, including Israel. In Matthew 11, Jesus acknowledges John the Baptist's ministry that preceded His own and was marked by violence in the name of God. Jesus highlights these violent tendencies of the past era, emphasizing that they did not reflect the true character of God. As we'll later discover, God is not violent but embodies peace, goodness, and kindness, which lead humanity to repentance.

But now you must put them all away: anger, wrath, malice, slander, and obscene talk from your mouth. Do not lie to one another, seeing that you have put off the old self with its practices and have put on the new self, which is being renewed in knowledge after the image of its creator. —Colossians 3:8-10

When we contemplate the third beatitude, we see that the divine Godhead exhibits supreme yet unoppressive power. Instead, its power is demonstrated through selfless, sacrificial love, which is synonymous with the essence of the Godhead Himself. While there was a time when violence may have seemed justified in the name of God, Jesus revealed such actions to be both unwise and inconsistent with His teachings. Ultimately, love prevails in all circumstances.

Beatitude Four: Blessed Are Those Who Hunger and Thirst for Righteousness

Romans 5:17 declares, "For if, by the trespass of the one man, death reigned through that one man, how much more will those who receive God's abundant provision of grace and of the gift of righteousness reign in life through the one man, Jesus Christ!"

The gift of righteousness can be seen as the initial grace that enables the believer to embark on the journey of *theosis*. It provides the necessary foundation of walking in the revelation of righteousness, which is essential for the transformative process of walking in union with Him. Both concepts, though articulated differently in various Christian traditions, ultimately converge in the believer's ongoing transformation and union with God. *Theosis* refers to the process of taking on God's nature, as described in 2 Peter 1:3-4. These verses highlight that God's divine power grants us everything we need for life and godliness, allowing us to partake in His nature. This concept suggests that we can become more like God without ceasing to be ourselves, experiencing a transformation that elevates us beyond our previous state. This process has nothing to do with outward acts of righteousness nor is it born from any act of man; it is the gift of God.

There's a distinction between God's indwelling and His reshaping of us. We're not just conformed to the image of Christ but transformed from glory to glory, taking on His righteousness and likeness. This transformation extends even to our physical bodies, resembling the resurrected Christ. It's a complete overhaul, making us increasingly like God. This is the fruit and the purpose of being in union with Christ.

Theosis, or maturing in righteousness, also known as deification, is a concept of salvation rooted in the belief that humanity's ultimate destiny is to be united with God. The idea of "becoming God" is central to this view, particularly in the teachings of the early church fathers, especially in the Greek tradition. The Orthodox doctrine of divinization, or *Theosis*, is considered a significant contribution of the Eastern church to Western theology, although it has often been overlooked or even rejected. According to Eastern fathers, humans can experience genuine and transformative union with God, which is seen as the ultimate purpose of human existence and the essence of salvation, both in the present and in the future. *Theosis* involves the participation of creation, especially the human soul, in divine deification or divinization, which can occur consciously and lovingly.

In contemplation of the fourth beatitude, we understand that the divine Godhead exemplifies and originates all righteousness. While Adam's actions led to death for all, the profound gift of righteousness far surpasses this, dispelling the delusion of separation and revealing humanity's unity with Christ.

Beatitude Five: Blessed Are the Merciful

Displaying mercy towards others isn't a means to gain entry into the kingdom; instead, it reflects a heart disposition that welcomes the mercy Jesus extends through His gospel message of the kingdom. Jesus's followers understand from this beatitude that God has always emphasized mercy as a fundamental requirement. Micah's timeless words echo this sentiment: "He has shown you, O mortal, what is good. And what does the LORD require of you? To act justly and to love mercy and to walk humbly with your God" (Micah 6:8, NIV).

> MERCY ISN'T JUST AN OCCASIONAL ACTION OF GOD; IT'S AN INTRINSIC PART OF GOD'S NATURE.

I am deeply convinced that mercy and forgiveness encompass the entirety of the gospel. The Benedictus (see Luke 1:68-79) affirms that salvation comes through the forgiveness of sin (Luke 1:77). Experiencing forgiveness or mercy reveals the boundless love of a gracious God, given freely without expectation of reciprocation. There's no exchange of favors. Grace cannot be purchased. Jesus symbolized this when He overturned the tables in the temple. One cannot earn God's favor through worthiness, accomplishments, or obedience to commandments. Salvation is a manifestation of God's enduring kindness, a kindness that endures "forever" (see Psalm 136), and beautifully illustrates God's unwavering mercy.

Mercy isn't just an occasional action of God; it's an intrinsic part of God's nature. Jesus emphasized this when He said, "I desire mercy, not sacrifice" (Matthew 9:13; 12:7, NIV). In Hebrew, the term used is *chesed*, representing a steadfast, enduring love that is unbreakable. This love is often translated as "loving-kindness" or "covenant love." God has established an unbreakable covenant with creation, and His love remains steadfast. It's ingrained in our divine image. However, instead of embracing divine mercy, we often cling to our sins and punish ourselves, refusing to accept forgiveness out of pride. Only the humble—the meek—can fully embrace and live in mercy.

In contemplating the fifth beatitude, we are shown that our holiness doesn't come from our own efforts but from countless acts of surrender to mercy. The essence of this beatitude lies in this realization. As we continually receive forgiveness throughout our lives, we are transformed into vessels of mercy. We embody what we accept into our hearts. Mercy becomes our driving force and our mission. True enlightenment and freedom come when we can both receive and extend mercy freely, without expecting payment or punishment in return.

Beatitude Six: Blessed Are the Pure in Heart

In ancient sacred traditions, the heart holds a distinct and perhaps unexpected significance. It's not merely the center of our emotions or personal identity, but rather an instrument for perceiving divine purpose and beauty. Consider it our antenna, guiding us toward divine radiance and aligning our essence with its subtle rhythms. Rather than being a vessel for personal expression, the heart is designed for divine perception.

Jesus declares in Matthew 5:8, "Blessed are the pure in heart, for they shall see God." When the heart is right, Jesus says our seeing will be right. He ties heart and sight together. Consider the saying, "Beauty is in the eyes of the beholder." So is God. All we need to do is keep the lens clean and the heart pure. Perhaps Jesus was alluding to this when He spoke of the purity of heart in His teachings. This purity involves having intentions, desires, and motivations that transcend self-interest—no longer concerned with personal image or seeking approval. Throughout the day, we must continually purify our intentions: "Why am I doing this?" When our intentions are rooted in compassionate love, centered in the heart, our actions become selfless and others-focused. We're drawn to those who embody such love, feeling comforted and softened in their presence.

In contemplation of the sixth beatitude, we see that the essence of purity emanates from the divine Godhead, serving as both its embodiment and origin. Through purity of heart, God perceives and engages with us, His beloved children. This purity isn't about establishing a culture we label as pure; rather, it involves embodying selfless love, or agape, towards all of humanity. It's a privilege for us to nurture and extend this purity to others.

Beatitude Seven: Blessed Are the Peacemakers

Peace is a significant aspect of the kingdom of God, comprising one-third of its essence, as outlined in Romans 14:17. Additionally, God is referred to as the Prince of Peace, as stated in Isaiah 9:6. Jesus exemplified nonviolent and peaceful actions in both His teachings and His life. He urges us to "turn the other cheek" and refrain from responding to vengeance with more vengeance. True peace can only be attained through the pursuit of peacemaking. However, some believe that peace can be achieved through violence, adopting the mindset of "stop killing by killing." This approach contradicts the teachings of all major religious figures throughout history.

Jesus cautions us that we will face opposition and hatred from various quarters. When we operate outside established systems and advocate for peace, we won't garner admiration from those within those systems. Instead, we may be viewed as dangerous, subversive, and unpatriotic. Jesus wasn't aligned with any particular nation; He served a much greater kingdom.

To truly embody peacemaking, one must embrace nonviolence and advocate for life at all stages, from conception to death. Unfortunately, many Christians today reserve the right to choose when, where, and with whom they will advocate for life and peace. They may justify the death penalty as a form of justice if they deem someone as wrong, guilty, unworthy, or sinful. However, this contradicts Jesus's ethical message: we cannot claim sole authority over life and death, as life originates from God and bears the divine image. True peacemaking requires a spiritual discernment that transcends political ideologies.

As we contemplate the seventh beatitude, we recognize that the Divine Father reigns as the Prince of Peace, offering a peace that transcends worldly understanding. In His kingdom, violence gives way to abundance, where swords are unnecessary and plowshares plentiful. Father, grant us the grace to embody peacemaking in a world still ensnared by the allure of violence.

Beatitude Eight: Blessed Are Those Who Are Persecuted for Righteousness

The eighth beatitude clarifies that the Beatitudes are neither prerequisites for entering the kingdom of God nor strict moral obligations. If they were, Jesus would endorse seeking persecution or martyrdom for divine favor. Instead, He consoles those unjustly persecuted, affirming their belonging in the kingdom. Jesus underscores this in His subsequent statement where He reassures those insulted or persecuted that despite appearances, the kingdom is theirs—a cause for genuine rejoicing.

> **THOSE WHO ARE MOCKED AND SLANDERED FIND JOY IN THE KINGDOM.**

In this beatitude, Jesus isn't referring to martyrdom but rather to a profound sense of liberation. The Gospel of Thomas offers a variation that encapsulates Jesus's message: "Blessed are you in the midst of persecution who, when they hate and pursue you even to the core of your being, cannot find 'you' anywhere." The Beatitudes lead us to a death of our selfish ambitions and a realization of our true selves in Christ Jesus. Through this awakening, we glimpse the eternal life of God in its true essence.

As we contemplate the eighth beatitude, we are shown a profound truth: those who are mocked and slandered find joy in the kingdom. Humility, simplicity, and strength of God's essence—not human prestige—define the kingdom of heaven. Embracing vulnerability, like our heavenly Father, contrasts with the world's pursuit of dominance. We exist in the world but remain distinct from its values.

RE-IMAGING GOD

While this chapter doesn't cover all the wisdom found in the Sermon on the Mount, I hope it offers profound insight into the eternal and unchanging character of God. The message of the Beatitudes challenged the religious leaders of the time because it contrasted sharply with their long-held perceptions of God. At the same time, it was a source of hope and encouragement for the misfits, outcasts, and marginalized, revealing a God who was far more compassionate and approachable than they had ever imagined.

Through the revelation of Jesus, they discovered a God who embodied qualities they had never seen nor envisioned. They found a Creator who, despite His immense power, identified with the poor in spirit. They encountered a God who empathized with human suffering and wept alongside them. They met a God whose gentleness contradicted the violent portrayals attributed to Him in Israel's history. This God freely offered righteousness as a gift, displayed unwavering mercy, and radiated purity of heart and peace. It was a stark contrast to the fearful and wrathful image humanity had been taught to fear. This was the God revealed through Jesus, hidden behind the Rorschach images projected onto Him. This was the God who looks like Jesus.

CHAPTER 6

WHAT ABOUT THE VIOLENT GOD?

There's certainly no denying that the Bible, the Old Testament especially, is full of horrifically violent images. We have examples such as Cain murdering Abel, Noah's flood, copious amounts of animal sacrifices, slavery, and the overwhelming cruelty and collateral damage of long-lasting campaigns of war. At surface level, we could agree that this is how humanity always prefers to advance itself, but it's particularly problematic in Scripture when we see God Himself commanding such acts. There then exists a dramatic tension that confronts every Christian believer and interpreter of Scripture. On the one hand, we encounter Old Testament stories of God seeming to command horrendous acts of violence. On the other hand, we read the unequivocally nonviolent teachings of Jesus in the New Testament. Reconciling these two has challenged Christians and theologians for two millennia.

The Old Testament narrates Israel's journey of discovering their God, an evolving process that shapes their understanding. While God remains unchanged, Israel's perception of Him evolves, leading to certain assumptions, like attributing violent characteristics to God akin to pagan deities. Over time, prophets like

Hosea challenge these assumptions, asserting that God desires mercy, not sacrifices—a notion Jesus echoed in His teachings.

> **BETWEEN THE APPARENT DIVINE SANCTION OF GENOCIDE IN THE CONQUEST OF CANAAN AND THE SERMON ON THE MOUNT, THERE'S A SIGNIFICANT SHIFT. IT'S NOT A CHANGE IN GOD BUT IN HUMANITY'S REVELATION OF HIS TRUE NATURE.**

Between the apparent divine sanction of genocide in the conquest of Canaan and the Sermon on the Mount, there's a significant shift. It's not a change in God but in humanity's revelation of His true nature. The Old Testament recounts Israel's journey to understanding God, but the journey doesn't end there—it leads to Jesus. Joshua and David offer glimpses, but it's Jesus of Nazareth who provides the full revelation of God. David was a product of his time, but Jesus, as the Son of David, embodies the exact nature of God.

Viewing the cross as a mirror allows you to see beyond the surface of violent depictions of God in the Old Testament. It unveils the true nature of God, fully revealed in Jesus Christ. If you struggle to reconcile the violent portrayals of God in the Old Testament with the message of the cross, it may indicate a lack of trust in the full revelation of God through Jesus. Previous glimpses of truth were obscured, suggesting an incomplete understanding of God's character prior to Jesus.

Violent depictions of God in the Old Testament serve as precursors to the crucified God. In essence, these violent portrayals can be seen as literary crucifixes, offering glimpses of the historical crucifixion when viewed through the lens of the cross.

OLD TESTAMENT "PROPHETIC" VIOLENCE

Let's take a look at Jeremiah's portrayal of God, where it seems like mercy and compassion are cast aside for the sake of destructive actions (see Jeremiah 13:14). But if we believe that the cross shows us who God really is, then we know that God would never abandon mercy and compassion to bring harm to families. So, we have to recognize that this grim image of God reflects Jeremiah's own flawed, culturally influenced understanding, rather than the true nature of God.

A significant portion of Jeremiah's ministry involved delivering what he perceived as divine judgment upon Israel. Throughout his prophetic messages, Jeremiah shared over one hundred disturbing images. While some of these images could potentially be interpreted as less grisly, many others appear to be quite explicit. Did God truly bring judgment upon children (see Jeremiah 2:30)? Did He intend to destroy everyone (see Jeremiah 6:21)? Did God provide poisoned water for the people to drink (see Jeremiah 8:14)? Did He want parents to resort to eating their own children out of desperation (see Jeremiah 19:7-9)? These questions highlight just a few examples of the violent and gruesome imagery associated with God in Jeremiah's prophecies. How can we reconcile such horrific imagery with the notion of a Christlike God? Can we find the God who looks like Jesus shining through such darkness?

Jeremiah 7:21-23 says:

> *Thus says the LORD of hosts, the God of Israel: "Add your burnt offerings to your sacrifices, and eat the flesh. For in the day that I brought them out of the land of Egypt, I did not speak to your fathers or command them concerning burnt offerings and sacrifices. But this command I gave them: 'Obey my voice, and I will be your God, and you shall be my people. And walk in all the way that I command you, that it may be well with you.'"*

In the middle of a book filled with gruesome depictions of violence attributed to God, there emerges a poignant reminder of what His heart truly desires for Israel. These unsettling images serve as a stark contrast, emphasizing that God's ultimate longing is for His people to know they are His beloved, they are cherished, and they are most fulfilled when intimately connected with Him. Sacrifice was never His desire, nor did He ever command it. Though the above reference may pertain to animal offerings, it's reasonable to infer that humans were never meant to be sacrificial pawns either.

Our trust in the God revealed on the cross flips these violent and disturbing portraits into a two-way mirror. When viewed in the light of the cross, we can see beyond these grim reflections of sin to witness the compassionate God embracing Jeremiah's flawed perception of Him. This is why God assumes this unpleasant appearance in Jeremiah's depiction in the Bible. Seen through the lens of the cross, violent portrayals of God, such as Jeremiah's, become both captivating and unsettling. These images are captivating because they reveal God bearing the weight of the sinful images we impose upon Him. Yet, they are also unsettling, as they challenge our projected beliefs about what God is capable of and willing to do to His beloved creation.

Another example we'll explore is that of the prophet Samuel and his complex connection with violence. Samuel faced the challenging task of anointing Saul, the first and one of the least successful kings in Israel's history. He also played a significant role in the reign of King David, one of Israel's most celebrated kings. Despite their differences, violence saturated both kings' reigns. I have no doubt that Saul and David viewed violence as a means of conquest, but how significant was the role of Samuel in the bloodshed we see attributed to God throughout these narratives?

PERHAPS WE ASSUME THAT AS A PROPHET OF GOD, SAMUEL'S ACTIONS REFLECT GOD'S WILL, EVEN WHEN THEY CONTRADICT CHRISTLIKE BEHAVIOR.

Throughout Samuel's prophetic tenure, it's evident how challenging it was for him to bear the burdens of the Israelites, Saul, and even David. While it's natural to feel anger, it becomes concerning when anger escalates to violence. Yet, we often overlook these questionable actions. Perhaps we assume that as a prophet of God, Samuel's actions reflect God's will, even when they contradict Christlike behavior. This is one of the primary problems we have when we don't interpret such images through the work of the cross and the Person of Jesus.

> Then Samuel said, "Bring me Agag, the king of the Amalekites." And Agag came to him cheerfully. And Agag said, "Surely the bitterness of death is gone!" But Samuel said, "As your sword has made women childless, so shall your mother be childless among women." And Samuel cut Agag to pieces before the LORD at Gilgal. —1 Samuel 15:32-33 (NASB)

What are your thoughts when you read the above verse? How do you feel about the prophet of God cutting a man into pieces? Now, you may reason that his actions are justified, and you may be right. You may also conclude that this wasn't God who did it, but it could still be viewed as a righteous act of justice against Agag. We might also observe that while it doesn't appear God commanded the killing of Agag, He was apparently okay with it since He didn't restrain Samuel and bore witness to it. Did Samuel have a violent streak, or was it God who had been violent all along?

Alright, full disclosure, maybe I'm just throwing you a curveball here. Perhaps you could justify this kind of horror if I provided a bit more context. What if I told you that Judges 3:13 shows that the Amalekites, along with their Moabite and Ammonite allies, defeated Israel to oppress them? Judges 10:11-13 also confirms that the Amalekites were among the oppressors of Israel. Additionally, Judges 6:1-6 reveals that the Amalekites, along with their Midianite allies, destroyed Israelite farms "as far as Gaza," leading to a famine. Surely, knowing this history should at least offer some context for Samuel's anger and desire for vengeance.

Understanding the historical atrocities that the Amalekites inflicted upon Israel sheds light on what appears to be God's command for their destruction through righteous vengeance. In fact, Samuel prophesied these commands and attributed them to God!

1 Samuel 15:2-3:

Thus says the LORD of hosts, "I have noted what Amalek did to Israel in opposing them on the way when they came up out of Egypt. Now go and strike Amalek and devote to destruction all that they have. Do not spare them, but kill both man and woman, child and infant, ox and sheep, camel and donkey."

Here's a more comprehensive understanding of the situation: Amalek had a long history of persecuting Israel, and Samuel prophesied that it was time for them to face severe consequences. As you continue reading 1 Samuel 15, you discover that Saul failed to fully carry out God's command. Instead of completely destroying everything as instructed, he spared King Agag and allowed his people to keep some of the spoils of war to offer as sacrifices to God at Gilgal. Saul's disobedience, including sparing Agag and preserving spoils, ultimately leads to the gruesome fate of Agag and the permanent separation of Samuel from Saul.

All things considered, where do we see the character and nature of God that looks like Jesus in this story? I submit that we see Him everywhere. We see Him bearing the image of sin in 1 Samuel 15:2-3 when it's attributed to Him as commanding the destruction of men, women, children, and animals. This is the image of God being crucified. We also see God in 1 Samuel 15:32-33 when He continues to lovingly work with Samuel despite his murderous actions exacted on Agag in the presence of God. But where else can we see the character and nature of the Christlike God in this story? Between Samuel's decree, attributed to the desire of God, and Agag's being hacked into pieces at the hands of Samuel, we find a gentle and soft ray of light breaking through the oppressive cloud of judgment and killing, resembling the God revealed through the Person of Jesus.

1 Samuel 15:21-22 (NIV):

> *The soldiers took sheep and cattle from the plunder, the best of what was devoted to God, in order to sacrifice them to the Lord your God at Gilgal. But Samuel replied: "Does the LORD delight in burnt offerings and sacrifices as much as in obeying the LORD? To obey is better than sacrifice, and to heed is better than the fat of rams."*

In these two verses, placed between grotesque acts of violence, the voice of God shines through. He expresses no interest or delight in burnt offerings and sacrifices. His love extends to all that He has created, and His desire is for relational intimacy. The Father reminds us that "to obey is better" and "to heed is better." However, since Samuel and the Israelites show absolutely no interest in these gentle reminders, they immediately resort to using senseless violence to resolve conflicts. This does not reflect the heart of God, yet He continues to patiently work with them, meeting them where they are and addressing their beliefs about what they believe He desires.

Similarly, just as we witness God bearing the weight of the violent descriptions that Jeremiah prophesied, allowing Himself to be portrayed in various acts of unimaginable violence, we observe a similar dynamic in the accounts involving Samuel. If we remain faithful to a "Jesus Hermeneutic," we see God's people making Him responsible for the violence we crave. We also witness Him acting upon us when He bears these distorted images to move us forward in our understanding of His nature until we finally behold the pure image bearer who is Jesus. Simply stated, the violent and vengeful God looks like our "Rorschach Imagery," and the kind, loving, compassionate, and non-violent God is the true image revealed through Jesus.

IF WE REMAIN FAITHFUL TO A "JESUS HERMENEUTIC," WE SEE GOD'S PEOPLE MAKING HIM RESPONSIBLE FOR THE VIOLENCE WE CRAVE.

VIOLENCE REPRODUCES VIOLENCE

We've caught a glimpse into the violent lifestyle and prophetic ministry of Samuel, but have you ever thought about how such violence can potentially impact others? Consider this: the two kings Samuel had direct ministerial influence over—Saul and David—were very violent men. Is this coincidence? It could be. But consider the words of Jesus in Matthew 26:52 when the Roman soldiers arrested Him, "Put your sword back into its place. For all who take the sword will perish by the sword" (NKJV). At this moment we would protest that Jesus had every right to defend Himself, but Jesus demonstrates the clear character and nature of God to His disciples that violence never stops violence.

In light of this truth, it's at least fair to question how much the violent streak in Samuel affected those he was most influential over. The kingship of Saul was saturated with violence, and we may think that since Saul wasn't technically God's idea, Israel got what she deserved. But this train of thought is hard to maintain when we know that David, God's anointed and chosen king, was much more violent than Saul. Let's make sure that we're tracking together: Saul was violent, but not chosen by God; David was much more violent but was chosen by God. What are we to do about this apparent paradox? What did Saul and David have in common? Samuel.

> "'Saul has slain his thousands, And David his ten thousands.' Then Saul became very angry, for this lyric displeased him; and he said, 'They have given David credit for ten thousands, but to me they have given credit for only thousands!'"—1 Samuel 18:7-8 (NASB)

I'm not claiming that Saul and David weren't responsible for their own actions—quite the opposite. I'm also not claiming that Samuel had some kind of nefarious spell over these men. But I do find it very interesting that people who have a propensity for violence tend to be attracted, empowered, and endeared to one another. Jesus, the perfect image of God, confronted Peter's violent streak time and time again. However, neither Saul, David, nor Samuel had enough clarity to break the cycle of their violent imagery.

VIOLENCE HAS A COST

Towards the end of King David's life, we witness a poignant exchange with his beloved son Solomon. In 1 Chronicles 22:7-9, David confides:

"My son, I had it in my heart to build a house for the name of the LORD my God. But the word of the LORD came to me, saying, 'You have shed much blood and have waged great wars. You shall not build a house to my name, because you have shed so much blood before me on the earth. Behold, a son shall be born to you who shall be a man of rest. . . . his name shall be Solomon, and I will give peace and quiet to Israel in his days.'"

When I was growing up, I idolized David to some extent. What wasn't to admire? He was a man's man! A warrior, a womanizer, a king, but also a worshiper, and ultimately, regarded as a man after God's own heart (see Acts 13:22). He expanded Israel's territory like no other before him and was widely hailed as the greatest king in their history. Jesus quoted him. Jesus even referred to him as His father. Such praise! Such accolades! But, when all is said and done, is this what David truly desired to achieve or be remembered for?

WOULD GOD COMMAND HIS BELOVED DAVID TO COMMIT ATROCITIES THAT WOULD DISQUALIFY HIM FROM FULFILLING THE DESIRE OF HIS HEART?

David's aspiration was to construct a house for God, a cherished dream he longed to fulfill. However, God conveyed that due to David's history of violent conquests, he would not be the one to build it. This raises a perplexing question: didn't God want

David to vanquish Israel's foes? While there are instances where God may not have directly commanded David to engage in violence, His silence and apparent blessings may lead one to interpret David's actions as divinely endorsed. Would God command His beloved David to commit atrocities that would disqualify him from fulfilling the desire of his heart? Here, I believe, we catch a glimpse of the true character and nature of God. He is not a God of war but of peace.

> *We cannot help Jesus repair the world and build the true house of the Lord if we remain fascinated with the violent ways of David the warlord. It's David the worshiper that God makes his covenant with, not David the warlord. The warlord cannot build the house of the Lord. It's David's peaceable Son who builds the true temple.*[18]

DO YOU IDENTIFY MORE WITH THE LION OR THE LAMB?

When it comes to prophetic symbolism representing Jesus, two images stand far above the rest: the lion and the lamb. Which image do you most identify with? Which image most excites you? For me, it was easy—I loved the Lion of the tribe of Judah all the way. I adored everything about the imagery—the majestic mane, the large claws, the roar, the sharp teeth, all of it. I had an appreciation for the lamb too; after all, it was the lamb that took away the sin of the world. But now that the lamb has been crucified, resurrected, and ascended, are we not living in the age of the lion? Right?

---

18 Brian Zahnd, "God Doesn't Build His House by Violence," *Brian Zahnd*, 1 Feb. 2013, https://brianzahnd.com/2012/12/god-doesnt-build-his-house-by-violence/.

Is Jesus alluded to as a lion? Certainly. When you examine Genesis 49:8-12, what do you envision for this descendant of Judah? He will receive praise from all. He will embody the strength of a lion, ruling over all peoples and crushing His enemies. Even His brothers will bow down to Him in reverence. His kingdom will be eternal, unchallenged by any other, and all nations will eventually bring tribute and worship before Him. He is the one to whom all nations owe obedience. Pair these thoughts with the imagery John penned in Revelation 5:5: "Stop weeping; behold, the Lion that is from the tribe of Judah, the Root of David, has overcome" (NASB).

Is Jesus alluded to as a lamb? Certainly. John the Baptist publicly declared in John 1:29, "Behold, the Lamb of God, who takes away the sin of the world!" John echoes the same declaration a little later when he encounters Jesus publicly. The prophet Isaiah declared lamb imagery, reflecting the crucifixion, hundreds of years before the incarnation had occurred when he said in Isaiah 53:7, "He [Jesus] was oppressed, and he was afflicted, yet he opened not his mouth; like a lamb that is led to the slaughter, and like a sheep that before its shearers is silent, so he opened not his mouth"

There's no way around it; Jesus is both the Lion and the Lamb. But how do we identify with both of these images and the tension they represent? The first challenge we face is how not to impose our own expectations on either image. When we behold the lion imagery, we must resist defaulting to a great apex predator that tears its enemies to pieces. Similarly, when we contemplate the lamb imagery, we must resist defaulting to simply a weak and defenseless pet. Again, both images are true of Jesus, but it is His image and not our own projections of it that should define Him.

I believe one of the clearest ways to see the images at rest together is found in John's prophetic vision in Revelation 5:5-6:

> And one of the elders said to me, "Weep no more; behold, the Lion of the tribe of Judah, the Root of David, has conquered, so that he can open the scroll and its seven seals." And between the throne and the four living creatures and among the elders I saw a Lamb standing, as though it had been slain.

In this vision of Jesus Christ, we behold the lion and the lamb, but it's worth noting that John only heard the decree that the lion was present, yet he only saw a lamb, as though it had been slain. What do these images mean?

THE LION CONQUERS AS THE CRUCIFIED LAMB. THIS IS WHO GOD HAS ALWAYS BEEN.

Jesus, being the Lion of the Tribe of Judah, represents His authority. It's true that His kingdom will be eternal, and all nations will bow their knee and declare that He is Lord. But how is this accomplished? Unbelievably, and contrary to our default methodology of violence, the Lion rules by being a slaughtered Lamb. The King of kings lays down His life and baptizes the world with other-centered, self-sacrificial agape to demonstrate the essence of His Kingship. The Lion conquers as the crucified Lamb. This is who God has always been.

MY KINGDOM IS NOT OF THIS WORLD

I want to make one more point in this chapter concerning the Godhead's non-violent way when it comes to our desire for power and empire-building. Jesus had a couple of very specific moments just before His crucifixion to speak to our perceived need for violence to defend ourselves or, at the very least, to defend Him: Peter cutting off the ear of Malchus and the conversation between Jesus and Pilate. The first example speaks to our personal need to take up arms to defend ourselves and others. The second example speaks to the temptation of marrying the gospel to the ways of empire.

THE FINAL MIRACLE JESUS PERFORMED BEFORE HIS CRUCIFIXION WAS HEALING SOMEONE WHO HATED HIM, DESPITE THAT PERSON BEING WOUNDED BY THE HANDS OF SOMEONE WHO LOVED HIM.

The backdrop for Peter cutting off the ear of Malchus is pretty straightforward (see John 18). Judas had just betrayed Jesus, taking the first substantial step toward His crucifixion. Witnessing this completely unjust betrayal, Peter, one of the disciples who had heard the Sermon on the Mount and knew the ways of Jesus's love and forgiveness firsthand, drew his sword and did what most of us would've done as well—he started defending his Lord through violence. While blood was surely flowing from the head of Malchus, Jesus completely overturned this act of violence by the hand of His disciple. He healed and restored a man who wanted to see Him imprisoned at best and crucified at worst.

Consider this: the final miracle Jesus performed before His crucifixion was healing someone who hated Him, despite that person being wounded by the hands of someone who loved Him. This wasn't simply an isolated incident of Jesus resigning to His fate but rather demonstrating the core of His lived gospel, as well as offering another example of redeeming the distorted "Rorschach Imagery" projected onto His Father for thousands of years. God never needed anyone fighting for Him, nor did He desire anyone to perpetrate violence on another. He would rather heal and restore than destroy, always.

The backdrop for the conversation between Jesus and Pilate can be found in all four Gospels. In John's account, we see Pilate speaking in the language of empire, which is the only language he knows. In John 18:33, Pilate asks the question that frames our perspective of two completely different systems of government: "Are you the king of the Jews?" (NIV) Asking this simple question is loaded with consequences. You see, Jerusalem had a king, and it wasn't Jesus; it was Herod. Any other king was a threat to his rule and therefore had to be exterminated.

When given the chance to respond, Jesus didn't answer Pilate with the language of empire, not because Jesus was in any way afraid of what others might do to Him but because it gave Him the opportunity to proclaim truths about His nature and His kingdom that are completely opposed to the violent ways of empire-building that men employed. Jesus says in John 18:36, "My kingdom is not of this world. If my kingdom were of this world, my servants would have been fighting, that I might not be delivered over to the Jews. But my kingdom is not from the world." To calm Pilate's heart, Jesus tells him that His kingdom doesn't overcome with violence. This type of kingdom imagery was completely foolish to someone like Pilate. Let's be honest, it's completely foolish to our modern sensibilities as well.

WE ARE QUICK TO FIGHT, BOTH LITERALLY AND CONVERSATIONALLY; WE PRAISE WARS WHEN WE DEEM THEM AS JUSTIFIED, AND WE CRAVE THE MARRIAGE OF THE GOSPEL WITH THE AMERICAN EMPIRE.

Today, I frequently mourn how much violence is celebrated in our culture. And before you think I'm talking about the world, which should be a given, I'm actually talking about the prevailing violence you can find within the professing church! We are quick to fight, both literally and conversationally; we praise wars when we deem them as justified, and we crave the marriage of the gospel with the American Empire. This all goes against the spoken and lived gospel of Jesus. Thankfully, more people are beginning to see the image of God free from their own projections. Thankfully, there is hope for a generation who learn to war no more (see Isaiah 2:4). Thankfully, there is a fresh desire to put the god of war to rest once and for all.

CHAPTER 7

WHAT ABOUT THE GOD WHO CRAVES SACRIFICE?

We've already examined a couple of archetypal examples of sacrifice earlier in this book, such as the story of Abraham and Isaac, and Adam and Eve. The revelation of Abraham encountering *Jehovah Jireh* not only completely changed Abraham's presumptions about God concerning the desire for sacrifices but was also meant to reveal to us, once and for all, that God is always a giver and not a taker. The Godhead gives Themselves as a sacrifice for all mankind and takes this revelation to its ultimate fulfillment. However, it's somewhat disappointing that while followers of *Abba* denounced human sacrifice, they couldn't rid themselves of the deeply engrained desire to shed the blood of animals to please God and make atonement for their sins.

> I BELIEVE THAT THE SACRIFICIALLY SATURATED CULTURE OF EGYPT CERTAINLY IMPACTED THE ISRAELITES. HOW COULD IT NOT?

To help us understand how deeply ingrained sacrifice was for the ancient Israelites, it's worth contemplating where they observed and imitated such practices. Between the death of Joseph (see Genesis 50:26) and their deliverance by Moses in Exodus, it is believed that they were enslaved in Egypt for around four hundred years. I believe that the sacrificially saturated culture of Egypt certainly impacted the Israelites. How could it not? There were Israelites who were born, lived, and died in Egyptian captivity and likely thought such behavior commonplace in offerings to deities. In addition to the influence of Egypt on sacrificial practices, both human and animal sacrifices were common in nearly all the surrounding ancient Near Eastern cultures of that time period.

There's disagreement on exactly when Israel began offering sacrifices to God. Moses mentioned the need for sacrifice to Pharaoh in Exodus 8, even though there's no record of God demanding sacrifice from Israel at that time. So, where did Moses come up with this idea? With one or two isolated examples beforehand, it's widely accepted, and easy to believe, that the sacrificial focus of ancient Israel intensified shortly after Exodus 19 with the implementation of the sacrificial system instituted in Leviticus. This makes sense because the Mosaic law became the great veil of distortion that Israel placed over the face of God, and for whatever reason, the projected images they placed on God were saturated in blood.

We'll explore several examples in this chapter of people offering sacrifices to God. Some are offered when it appears God approves and enjoys, but there are also many instances when God has no use for them and only desires relational intimacy. As we navigate these opposing views, it's helpful to remember that these instances are saturated with culturally conditioned ideas of the deities' desires concerning sacrifices. These notions are then projected onto God, and He stoops down to their level of understanding, bearing their distorted "Rorschach Imagery" and working with them where they are. Each example serves as a literary crucifix on behalf of our always-good Father.

JEHOVAH > PAGAN GODS

There are numerous examples in the Old Testament of God distinguishing Himself from pagan gods. It's interesting to note that many of these distinctions revolve around the issue of sacrifice. For instance, we find God's declaration, in close proximity to the establishment of the sacrificial system of ancient Israel in Deuteronomy 32:37-38 (NIV): "Now where are their gods, the rock they took refuge in, the gods who ate the fat of their sacrifices and drank the wine of their drink offerings? Let them rise up to help you! Let them give you shelter!" If God was exactly like the pagan gods when it came to eating and drinking sacrifices, why make this distinction? I submit that this distinction is made because He stands apart from them altogether.

King David provides a clear example of the distinctions between what he wanted to offer to God as sacrifice and how God actually responded to those sacrifices. In 2 Samuel 24, we encounter the dramatic account of attributing to God the killing of seventy thousand men through a pestilence because David conducted a census to count the people of Israel. This event presents a distorted image of God. In an attempt to stop the pestilence, David decides to offer sacrifices to God. He offers to purchase the threshing floor of Araunah the Jebusite, where the angel causing the pestilence had stopped and was awaiting David's response. The issue is eventually resolved in 2 Samuel 24:24-25, where David declares, "I will not offer burnt offerings to the LORD my God that cost me nothing." Consequently, David buys the threshing floor and the oxen for fifty shekels of silver, builds an altar to the Lord, and offers burnt offerings and peace offerings. In response, the Lord relents from the plague, and it is averted from Israel.

If God truly required sacrifices to appease Him and prevent Him from causing destruction, let's contrast that with the words of Asaph, one of King David's trusted psalmists, in Psalm 50:9-15 (NIV). Asaph declares:

I have no need of a bull from your stall or of goats from your pens, for every animal of the forest is mine, and the cattle on a thousand hills. I know every bird in the mountains, and the insects in the fields are mine. If I were hungry I would not tell you, for the world is mine, and all that is in it. Do I eat the flesh of bulls or drink the blood of goats? Sacrifice thank offerings to God, fulfill your vows to the Most High, and call on me in the day of trouble; I will deliver you, and you will honor me.

This is a prime example of God making His desire known concerning sacrifices: He doesn't want them, nor does He need them. However, He also relents to our desire to sacrifice and still allows us to do what we want because we have a distorted image that sacrificing to Him allows us to be closer. What we perceive isn't true, but God bears it nonetheless.

OUTSIDE OF RELATIONSHIP, GOD TAKES NO PLEASURE IN WHAT WE OFFER.

In Psalm 51, the heart of David shines brightly and reflects the unveiled heart of God. These thoughts completely challenge much of what David has personally engaged in and give us much-needed perspective on what true "sacrifice" really is. David declares in Psalm 51:16-17 (NIV), "You do not delight in sacrifice, or I would bring it; you do not take pleasure in burnt offerings. My sacrifice, O God, is a broken spirit; a broken and contrite heart you, God will not despise." Do you see what God has always been after? He has always desired for us to have a broken spirit and a contrite heart. These are relationally intimate terms. Outside of relationship, God takes no pleasure in what we offer.

There are myriad other examples to consider where we see God dismissing and even chastising our useless sacrificial ways. Consider the prophetic word of Isaiah in Isaiah 1:11 (NIV) when he declares,

"The multitude of your sacrifices—what are they to me?" says the Lord. "I have more than enough of burnt offerings, of rams and the fat of fattened animals; I have no pleasure in the blood of bulls and lambs and goats."

Through the prophet Amos, God expresses His displeasure with sacrifices and the religious circus surrounding the spectacle when He declares in Amos 5:21-23 (NIV):

> "I hate, I despise your religious festivals; your assemblies are a stench to me. Even though you bring me burnt offerings and grain offerings, I will not accept them. Though you bring choice fellowship offerings, I will have no regard for them. Away with the noise of your songs! I will not listen to the music of your harps."

Even the prophet Jeremiah somehow taps into the heart of God right in the middle of some of the most horrific depictions of violence in the entirety of Scripture and utters these words from the heart of God in Jeremiah 7:21-23 (NKJV),

> Thus says the LORD of hosts, the God of Israel: "Add your burnt offerings to your sacrifices and eat meat. For I did not speak to your fathers, or command them in the day that I brought them out of the land of Egypt, concerning burnt offerings or sacrifices. But this is what I commanded them, saying, 'Obey My voice, and I will be your God, and you shall be My people. And walk in all the ways that I have commanded you, that it may be well with you.'"

This is a major revelation! God communicates that He never gave instructions to the ancient Israelites coming out of Egypt concerning burnt offerings or sacrifices. God never wanted sacrifices from us, but we built an entire system around our perceptions of a bloodthirsty god anyway. This is a prime example of what it means for God to bear the burden of our "Rorschach Imagery."

JESUS WEIGHS IN ON SACRIFICES

In Matthew 22 and Mark 12, we find Jesus being questioned about which commands of the old covenant were the greatest. Jesus responds to the question by quoting Deuteronomy 6:5, "You shall love the LORD your God with all your heart and with all your soul and with all your might." In the account of Matthew 22, Jesus makes it clear that He's not establishing new laws but summarizing what the old covenant poorly attempted to communicate. Of particular interest is how the scribe in Mark 12:33 adds to this declaration of Jesus, "And to love him with all the heart and with all the understanding and with all the strength, and to love one's neighbor as oneself, is much more than all whole burnt offerings and sacrifices." When the scribe concludes that love is greater than the sum of all burnt offerings and sacrifices, Jesus tells him, "You are not far off from the kingdom of God" (Mark 12:34).

The writer of Hebrews quotes Jesus as saying, "Sacrifices and offerings you have not desired, but a body have you prepared for me; in burnt offerings and sin offerings you have taken no pleasure" (Hebrews 10:5-6). Attributing this statement to Jesus is mystically beautiful! Jesus doesn't quote this anywhere in the accounts of the Gospels, but King David prophesied it in Psalm 40:6 when he declares, "In sacrifice and offering you have not delighted, but you have given me an open ear. Burnt offering and sin offering you have not required." The writer of Hebrews appropriated the prophetic song of David as the spoken words of the Christ.

There is no record of Jesus ever giving sacrifices, although it is possible. But first, we should consider that sacrifices were brought for the purposes of atonement (see Exodus 29:36), and He had no sins for which to atone. However, He also had no sins of which He needed to repent to receive remission, yet He submitted to John's "baptism of repentance for the remission of sins" (Mark 1:4, NKJV). Of course, we understand that He was baptized "to fulfill all righteousness" (Matthew 3:15). In other words, for us to be counted among the righteous, He had to be "numbered with the transgressors," so He could die for them (Isaiah 53:12). Thus, He was counted among the transgressors in His baptism, and also when He died between two transgressors (see Mark 15:28). But if He identified with sinners at the beginning of His ministry with His baptism, and at the end of His ministry with His death, perhaps He identified with sinners in between those events as well, through animal sacrifices.

WHAT WE DO KNOW IS TRUE FROM THE HEART OF JESUS IS THAT LOVING GOD AND OTHERS REIGN SUPREME ABOVE ALL SACRIFICIAL OFFERINGS.

It is certainly possible that Jesus may have participated in sacrifices as an act of human solidarity, but this in no way validates the practice or makes these sacrifices beneficial. If true, this thought is also steeped in the love and goodness of God. Imagine Jesus, who has no use or desire for sacrifices, still participating in them with His people because He wants to fully embrace the distorted imagery of blood sacrifice so that He might redeem it once and for all. What we do know is true from the heart of Jesus is that loving God and others reign supreme above all sacrificial offerings. Not only do Jesus's teachings challenge this notion, but they also find their ultimate culmination in His giving Himself as the true self-sacrificial Lamb who takes away the sin of the world.

SELF-SACRIFICIAL LAMB

"To look at Jesus—especially on the Cross, says 1 John—is to behold the clearest depiction of the God who is love (1 John 4:8). I've come to believe that Jesus alone is perfect theology."
—Brad Jersak[19]

Of the many mystical things accomplished through the work of the cross, Jesus redeems for us the entire sacrificial narrative. He is not offering a sacrifice to please His Father; They are present together in this divine act (see 2 Corinthians 5:19). Jesus isn't offering a sacrifice to draw closer to His Father; They are fully within the other (see John 14:20). Jesus isn't offering a sacrifice to atone for His sin as we discover in 2 Corinthians 5:21, "For our sake he made him to be sin who knew no sin, so that in him we might become the righteousness of God." Nothing about the self-sacrificial work of Jesus on the cross had anything to do with needing personal forgiveness. Jesus as the perfect sacrifice looked unrecognizable through the lens of the system attributed to Him.

> **JESUS AS THE PERFECT SACRIFICE LOOKED UNRECOGNIZABLE THROUGH THE LENS OF THE SYSTEM ATTRIBUTED TO HIM.**

---

[19] Bradley Jersak, *A More Christlike God: A More Beautiful Gospel* (Pasadena, CA: Plain Truth Ministries, March 28, 2016).

The self-sacrificial Lamb completely dismantled the notion of repetitive sacrifice, as we discover in Hebrews 10:12 and 14: "But when Christ had offered for all time a single sacrifice for sins, he sat down at the right hand of God. . . . For by a single offering he has perfected for all time those who are being sanctified." Through His self-sacrifice, Jesus dealt with the sin problem for all humanity (see Hebrews 10:17-18; 1 Peter 2:24). He also shattered the delusion of distance and separation between God and man, as we discover in 2 Corinthians 5:17-19:

> Therefore, if [since] anyone is in Christ, he is a new creation. The old has passed away; behold, the new has come. All this is from God, who through Christ reconciled us to himself and gave us the ministry of reconciliation; that is, in Christ God was reconciling the world to himself, not counting their trespasses against them, and entrusting to us the message of reconciliation.

At surface level, the cross was a vile, bloody, and sacrificial death. Jesus, in the natural, bore all the sin imagery that humanity could project on Him. Ponder this: when the first-century Jews beheld the crucified Christ "from a worldly perspective," similar to how Paul once viewed things, all they perceived was a condemned, God-cursed criminal—indistinguishable from the myriad others whom the Romans crucified. We can further recall these truths when we lean into the prophetic imagery of the prophet Isaiah when he declares of Jesus, "Just as there were many who were appalled at him—his appearance was so disfigured beyond that of any human being and his form marred beyond human likeness" (Isaiah 52:14, NIV).

> **THE CROSS WASN'T AN EVENT THAT IN ANY WAY CHANGED GOD'S MIND ABOUT US; RATHER, IT ULTIMATELY CHANGED OUR MINDS ABOUT HIM.**

The marred image of the self-sacrificial Lamb was our sin image, our projected "Rorschach Imagery" that our own broken experiences deeply influenced. Jesus appeared as one separated from God, but this was our distorted perspective. It seems God has cursed Him, but again, this was our distorted perspective. He resembled the wages of sin yet bore the sin of us all out of His profound and magnificent love for us. The cross is simultaneously ugly and beautiful, soft and savage. Jesus absorbed everything that represented fallen humankind in a single, horrific, and beautiful moment.

The cross wasn't an event that in any way changed God's mind about us; rather, it ultimately changed our minds about Him. The cross doesn't change God's character; it reveals it. This means that God has always been as the cross shows Him to be. Hebrews 13:8 emphasizes this, stating that Jesus Christ remains the same yesterday, today, and forever. The God shown on the cross is the same God who inspired Scripture to ultimately reveal Himself through the cross.

If you once believed that God had a "dark side," encountering the God revealed on Calvary might seem "too good to be true." If this happens, allow yourself to embrace the good news! However beautiful you imagine God to be, He is infinitely more beautiful than that! Feeling like it's "too good to be true" simply means you're moving in the right direction. This feeling arises because you may have grown accustomed to imagining God as "good," even though your previous image of God was partly flawed. As you continue to trust in the cross completely, your habit of associating truth with a flawed image of God will gradually fade away.

"Perhaps the most fundamental truth which we have to learn in the Christian Church, or rather relearn since we have suppressed it, is that the Incarnation was the coming of God to save us in the heart of our fallen and depraved humanity. . . . That is to say, the Incarnation is to be understood as the coming of God to take upon himself our fallen human nature, our actual human existence laden with sin and guilt, our humanity diseased in mind and soul in its estrangement or alienation from the Creator."—T. F. Torrance[20]

---

20 T. F. Torrance, *The Mediation of Christ* (Colorado Springs, CO: Helmers & Howard Publishing, 1992) 48-49.

CHAPTER 8

WHAT IS GOD'S IDEAL?

"The feeling remains that God is on the journey, too."
—Saint Teresa of Avila[21]

Human violence and sacrifices are the two main overarching themes of much of the Old Testament and are therefore what we see God challenge most directly through the revelation of His nature time and again. Now that we have examined these two major themes, we can more easily identify some other examples where God is trying to share His ideal within the fallen and distorted imaging of humanity. I find Greg Boyd's analogy of God as a heavenly missionary to humanity within our fallen and violent planet compelling in his book *Cross Vision*.[22] Because God's love for people cannot be a control mechanism (see 1 John 4:18), He gently works alongside and within our flawed understanding of Him, using His love to guide us toward a more Christlike expression of His ideals.

---

21 Lisa Fullam, "Oct. 15: Teresa of Avila," *Commonweal Magazine*, 15 Oct. 2009, www.commonwealmagazine.org/oct-15-teresa-avila.
22 Gregory A. Boyd, *Cross Vision: How the Crucifixion of Jesus Makes Sense of Old Testament Violence* (Minneapolis, MN: Fortress Press, August 15, 2017).

> **BECAUSE GOD'S LOVE FOR PEOPLE CANNOT BE A CONTROL MECHANISM (SEE 1 JOHN 4:18), HE GENTLY WORKS ALONGSIDE AND WITHIN OUR FLAWED UNDERSTANDING OF HIM, USING HIS LOVE TO GUIDE US TOWARD A MORE CHRISTLIKE EXPRESSION OF HIS IDEALS.**

God created people to be free, making them completely compatible with love. Since love is the opposite of fear, God often manifests as a loving influence rather than a coercive power. This means that God frequently finds Himself amidst our flawed delusions and distorted images of Him, bearing our sin imagery, so that He can gently guide us toward a deeper understanding of His ultimate character and nature. This journey of co-suffering with humanity is deeply heartbreaking for God and reveals His character and nature, as seen in Jesus's crucifixion on the cross. When we witness God bearing our "Rorschach Imagery," it reflects Him as a heavenly missionary rather than an ancient god of war.

There are many instances when God appears to be downright pagan as He bears our projected images of what we believe He is like. Remember, this doesn't mean that God changes to accommodate our actions, nor is He revealing anything about His nature that opposes Christ and Him crucified. When we stay committed to a Jesus hermeneutic and allow all our imaging of God to be revealed and defined through the self-sacrificial, other-centered *agape* of the crucified Christ, we can find our heavenly missionary working throughout the Scriptures.

GOD'S IDEAL FOR MARRIAGE

Marriage is the most sacred covenantal relationship within our human framework. It reflects the heart of other-centered, self-sacrificial love, as two independent lives become so intimately connected that they are recognized as one. We see God's ideal at the beginning of the Genesis narrative as we discover, "For this reason a man shall leave his father and his mother, and be joined to his wife; and they shall become one flesh" (Genesis 2:24, NASB). The writer of Hebrews declares, "Let marriage be held in honor among all" (Hebrews 13:4). The apostle Paul even compares the love between husband and wife to the love Jesus has for the church when he writes, "Husbands, love your wives, as Christ loved the church and gave himself up for her" (Ephesians 5:25).

God's ideal for marriage is fairly clear: two will be joined together as one flesh, the relationship is to be honored and valued, and the love between husband and wife has the power to reflect the profound love Jesus has for the church. That's a powerful ideal! However, it doesn't take long within the Scriptural narrative for us to see polygamy (the marrying of multiple spouses) running rampant. For example, in the story of Abraham, he married Sarah and Hagar, and likewise, we hear of Jacob marrying both Leah and Rachel. However, in both cases, while events are described, God did not instruct either Abraham or Jacob to marry multiple wives. God doesn't support polygamy, but He also doesn't appear to condone it. I submit this as an example of God working within the cultural conditions of Abraham and Jacob's time as a heavenly missionary, bearing their image, to lovingly influence them toward His ideal.

In addition to Abraham and Jacob having multiple wives, God never explicitly speaks out against leaders like Samuel, David, and Solomon having multiple wives. There are moments, at a surface level, when it appears that God is condoning polygamy, as seen in 2 Samuel 12:8 (NIV):

"I also gave you your master's house and put your master's wives into your care, and I gave you the house of Israel and Judah; and if that had been too little, I would have added to you many more things like these!"

This is an example of God "breathing" or allowing this verse to be included in the written record. Why? It serves as a reflection of our desires, not His ideals. That being understood, God allows our flawed perspective to remain in the story, not because He supports polygamy, but to show us over and over again that He loves us and works with us in the many places where we bear distorted perspectives of Him.

Outside of the institution of marriage, there are also multiple examples in the Bible of women being groomed as concubines. Concubines were women who bore men's children but were not officially married to them. God didn't encourage this practice, but He didn't condemn it either. So, do we assume that because God was silent on this issue, He was also complicit in it, or is there something else to be discovered in the behavior of our heavenly missionary? In the ancient Near East, women and children who were not under the protection of men were extremely vulnerable. Would it have done more harm or good during that time culturally for God to enforce His ideal of restricting sex to the marriage covenant? This isn't God compromising His character but rather sharing His loving nature to deter them from distorted cultural practices and draw them closer toward His ideal.

Nevertheless, even with God allowing all these non-ideal practices around marriage, men were still divorcing their wives, leaving them in vulnerable situations. Due to the hardness of the people's hearts, as Jesus mentioned (see Matthew 19:8), the heavenly missionary bore their sin imagery further, allowing for divorce and remarriage while establishing some humane rules to protect vulnerable women. Understanding the significance of this concession—permitting remarriage, despite Jesus's teaching that doing so technically involves adultery (see Matthew 5:32)—helps us grasp the magnitude of God's accommodation, even if it involves breaking one of the Ten Commandments prohibiting adultery.

GOD'S IDEAL FOR KINGSHIP

God desired to be the sole king, or more accurately the Father to whom humans submitted, hoping that His chosen people would serve as a model for other nations, demonstrating that they could thrive without human kings. We see God's heart expressed through His covenant with Abraham when He declares, "I will establish my covenant as an everlasting covenant between me and you and your descendants after you for the generations to come, to be your God and the God of your descendants after you" (Genesis 17:7, NIV). God desired relational intimacy, not a monarchy. This arrangement would have looked radically different from all the nations surrounding ancient Israel at that time.

As time passed, the nation of Israel demanded a king to lead them and fight their battles, following the example of other nations. They showed no interest in relational intimacy with God; instead, they sought a king from among their own people who would likely establish a monarchical system focused on conquest. Israel's request for a king dismayed Samuel (literally, it was "evil in his eyes"), so he prayed to God (see 1 Samuel 8:6). God instructed Samuel to heed the people's demand, clarifying, "Listen to all that the people are saying to you; it is not you they have rejected, but they have rejected me as their king" (1 Samuel 8:7, NIV). God further explained, "As they have done from the day I brought them up out of Egypt until this day, forsaking me and serving other gods, so they are doing to you" (1 Samuel 8:8, NIV). Throughout their history, Israel had been rebellious, consistently rejecting Jehovah and worshiping false gods.

GOD BEARING THE DESIRE OF MEN FOR THE LESSER IDEAL OF A KING FROM WITHIN THEIR OWN RANKS WAS A HUGE DEAL IN THE ANCIENT NEAR EAST.

After God relented to His people's demand, the biblical accounts consistently show God as approving, working through, and blessing Israel's kings, despite their initial rejection of Him. Even when the kings made mistakes and brought calamity upon the people, God never responded with "I told you so!" Instead, He continued to work through the institution of kingship, almost giving the impression that it was His idea all along. God bearing the desire of men for the lesser ideal of a king from within their own ranks was a huge deal in the ancient Near East. The monarchy, typically inherited by the king's eldest son, held a central role in the religion of surrounding nations to Israel. Each nation believed that its god selected and operated through their king and that the fate of the nation depended on the king's actions. Obedience to their deity led to blessings and victory in battle, while disobedience resulted in punishment and defeat.

Ultimately, Israel's request for a king stemmed from sinful motives; they desired to imitate the other nations rather than maintain their status as the holy (set apart) nation that God had designated them to be (see Exodus 19:6). This sinful demand led to the kingship serving as a form of judgment on them. By requesting a king to rule over them, God granted Israel's request, providing them with an earthly king who would act in his own interests. This is evident throughout Israel's history of monarchy, as their kings often pursued selfish agendas. Despite a few exceptions, the majority of Israel's kings were corrupt and oppressive, including the ideal king, David, who had his moral shortcomings. In many respects, the institution of monarchy served as a self-punishment for Israel.

God never explicitly approved or appointed kings; the ancient Israelites assumed that since God allowed their desire for kingship, He must now support any ensuing conquests. When we examine the multitude of violent depictions of God through the lens of the crucified Christ, we can discern that there's another aspect at play in the narratives of Israel's military triumphs (and failures)—something that the original inspired authors might not have fully grasped due to their limited understanding of God's true character and nature. This additional perspective clarifies that God never needed to resort to violence when advocating for Israel.

GOD'S IDEAL FOR "WAR"

The apostle Paul understood well the tension between living out the non-violent ways of God and residing in the midst of an extremely savage culture. Paul wasn't only victimized by his own people, the Jews, who stoned him (see Acts 14:9); the Romans also beat him with rods three times and eventually beheaded him under the order of Nero (see 2 Timothy 4:6-8). Once we understand the violence Paul endured, it's remarkable to hear him declare in 2 Corinthians 10:3, "For though we walk in the flesh, we are not waging war according to the flesh." At the very least, every Christian should embrace the truth that we do not fight or wage war in "fleshly" ways because we no longer live according to the flesh.

To suggest that we do not wage war does not, however, mean that we are helpless. Paul continues his train of thought concerning how to overcome fleshly violence: "For the weapons of our warfare are not of the flesh but have divine power to destroy strongholds" (2 Corinthians 10:4). This means that while war and violence may be used against us, retaliating in like manner is not what we are equipped to do. We do not engage in such warfare because, first, our heavenly Father never models or endorses such actions, and second, our "weapons" have no use in a conflict in which blood is being spilled. Our weapons are not for cutting off someone's ear but rather for transforming the hearts and minds of men.

Our weapons serve as effective tools for *metanoia*. This Greek word suggests more than simply changing WHAT others think; it serves to impact HOW people think. Paul also echoes this truth when he says, "We destroy arguments and every lofty opinion raised against the knowledge of God, and take every thought captive to obey Christ" (2 Corinthians 10:5). This is our warfare! We do not fight against others in the flesh; instead, we use the revelation of the crucified Christ to destroy any thinking that does not align with God's thoughts. As this transformation takes hold, it leads us to deep levels of our placement in Christ, thereby convincing us once and for all that we are not enemies but brothers.

Contrary to what we have traditionally believed about God, He would never endorse or encourage violence between any of His beloved children. This doesn't mean that God is passive when it comes to injustice or the need for correction, but it does mean that His methods do not reflect our desire to assert dominance or destroy enemies. Consider the unusual account in Deuteronomy 7:20-22 when Moses declares,

> *"Moreover, the LORD your God will send hornets among them, until those who are left and hide themselves from you are destroyed. You shall not be in dread of them, for the LORD your God is in your midst, a great and awesome God. The LORD your God will clear away these nations before you little by little."*

Is it possible that God would literally use bees to drive people out of the land meant for Israel slowly over time? Why not? This type of action appears to reflect the crucified Christ much more than the later declaration of Moses when the Israelites would encounter anyone worshiping false gods: "But you shall kill him. Your hand shall be first against him to put him to death, and afterward the hand of all the people" (Deuteronomy 13:9).

WHEN YOU BEGIN TO SEE IMAGES OF GOD THAT LOOK NOTHING LIKE JESUS, YOU ARE PERFECTLY FREE AND ENCOURAGED TO QUESTION WHAT YOU'RE READING.

Have you ever considered how God first dealt with the Egyptians' oppression of the ancient Israelites, setting the stage for their exodus? Each of the plagues mentioned in Exodus 6-11 looks nothing like God using the violence of the sword to influence Egypt to set Israel free. It's certainly not enjoyable to endure plagues such as water turning to blood, frogs, lice, flies, livestock pestilence, boils, hail, locusts, and extended darkness, but these are much better alternatives to the typical carnage involved in the overthrow of oppressors. But as these stories tend to unfold in the Old Testament, the God who is patiently influencing Pharaoh to set Israel free turns extremely violent and is attributed to killing, either personally or through the angel of death, the firstborn of all Egypt. Which influence looks more like the crucified Christ? I submit that allowing plagues to influence hard hearts to grant Israel freedom from oppression aligns much more closely with His character and nature than commanding the killing of the firstborn.

There are certainly many more instances we could examine to drive the point home, but I think you get the idea. When you begin to see images of God that look nothing like Jesus, you are perfectly free and encouraged to question what you're reading. Remember, disagreeing with the Bible is not the same as disagreeing with Jesus, to whom the Bible is meant to point us. Even when Scripture presents un-Christlike images of God that don't look like Jesus, I trust "I don't know" as the only answer I have to explain it more than applying a rigid interpretation of violent imagery to the God who is our always good Father:

> Father Richard Rohr proposes, "If you see God operating at a lesser level than the best person you know, then the text is not authentic revelation." If God is love (see 1 John 4:16), then no person could be more loving than God, Rohr says. "God is never less loving than the most loving person you know."[23]

Amen.

DOES GOD AT LEAST CHOOSE SIDES?

It seems that the more we are exposed to the unflinching goodness and kindness of God, the more desperate we become to look at least a little bit like God. If we believe that God never endorses or engages in violence, and His methods of influence look nothing like ours, and He is patient in the midst of anger and hostility imposed upon Him, do we have evidence to indicate that God at least chooses sides between those we feel are favored by Him and those we are convinced are not? I'm reminded of Joshua

---

23 John Buchanan, "The History Channel's Violent God," *The Christian Century*, 17 Apr. 2013, www.christiancentury.org/article/2013-03/bible-s-violent-god.

having an encounter with who many biblical scholars believe is the pre-incarnate Jesus, and Joshua asks, "Are you for us or for our enemies?" The Lord answers clearly and directly, "Neither" (Joshua 5:13). Can you believe this? The Lord refused to pick Israel over Jericho! How unlike us.

If it wasn't enough that the Lord wouldn't choose sides against Israel, let's take a look at the instructions delivered to Joshua for how to conquer the Canaanites. The Lord instructs Israel:

> "See, I have given Jericho into your hand, with its king and mighty men of valor. You shall march around the city, all the men of war going around the city once. Thus shall you do for six days. Seven priests shall bear seven trumpets of rams' horns before the ark. On the seventh day you shall march around the city seven times, and the priests shall blow the trumpets. And when they make a long blast with the ram's horn, when you hear the sound of the trumpet, then all the people shall shout with a great shout, and the wall of the city will fall down flat." —Joshua 6:2-5

The Lord's proposed strategy of "war" was marching in silence for days, blowing trumpets, and shouting. What kind of warfare is this? It sounds like the Lord was trying to show us, all the way back in the Old Testament, that the weapons of our warfare are not of the flesh, but of the spirit.

After the supernatural war strategy gained Israel a flawless victory, the story continues, yet again, as such stories tend to unfold. We see the Israelites take Jericho, and then Joshua declares, "The city and all that is within it shall be devoted to the LORD for destruction" (Joshua 6:17). And here we see, yet again, the

Rorschach God emerge from the story. Jericho was defeated in a non-violent, supernatural way because it reflected the God we behold through the crucified Christ. But once the walls of Jericho fell, the automatic response was violence and bloodshed devoted to God. God bears this distorted imagery from Joshua and Israel and continues to work with them at their level. Thank you, God, for such patience with us all!

> **HE'S NOT CHOOSING SIDES, BUT HE IS BINDING UP THE WOUNDED ON BOTH SIDES.**

In October 2023, I had the opportunity to record an episode on my podcast, *The Kingdom Is for Everyone*, discussing Hamas' surprise attack on Israel (Episode #61: "Israel and Hamas"). This episode continues to be one of my most popular, and the reasons likely vary, but the feedback I've gotten from the listeners is focused on this question: during the infighting between Israel and Hamas, where is Jesus? I explained that Jesus is a heavenly medic in the midst of the bloodshed. He's not choosing sides, but He is binding up the wounded on both sides. His heart breaks for any loss of life and any human suffering. When it comes to any of His children, which is all of us, Jesus doesn't choose sides.

CHAPTER 9
THE ENEMY'S TABLE

"Jesus came to tell men that they have no enemies but themselves."
—Blaise Pascal

In perhaps the most popular of all the Psalms, we find David singing of the Lord's comfort and companionship, even in the valley of the shadow of death. But the part of the song that I've been contemplating for a few years now is, "You prepare a table before me in the presence of my enemies; you anoint my head with oil; my cup overflows" (Psalm 23:5). When I read this growing up, I would imagine a great table with all my enemies sitting there, no meal or drink for them in sight. I, of course, was seated at the head of the table and had a tremendous feast in front of me. And while I was enjoying my meal, God was anointing me with favor. My enemies were tormented as they watched me enjoy the blessings of the Lord they were lacking. After all, I was a beloved son, and they were His enemies. Sigh.

It's amazing how much we can read ourselves into a scriptural text and allow our imaginations to construct the narrative. The two biggest issues with my interpretation of that scripture were that it assumed I wasn't an enemy of God and that God would anoint me as some form of humiliation for them. Those are two pretty big assumptions on my part! To think that I wasn't an enemy of God and that God, in all of His goodness, would humiliate others I viewed as enemies looks a lot more like I'm worshiping the God of my own making instead of the God who looks like Jesus.

> **THE WORDS OF JESUS CHALLENGE THE PERMISSION TO HUMILIATE OUR ENEMIES WHEN HE CLEARLY TEACHES AND LIVES LOVING OUR ENEMIES.**

This is another example of why we have to allow Jesus to clean the lens of our hearts and commit to living His way. Observing how Jesus treated enemies sitting at His table is a good place to start. Jesus is pretty clear in the Sermon on the Mount when He declares, "You have heard that it was said, 'You shall love your neighbor and hate your enemy.' But I say to you, Love your enemies and pray for those who persecute you, so that you may be sons of your Father who is in heaven" (Matthew 5:43-45). The words of Jesus challenge the permission to humiliate our enemies when He clearly teaches and lives loving our enemies.

These reflections on the lifestyle and teaching of Jesus caused me to land on a singular question—does God have enemies? If you go back and read Psalm 23 again, you'll notice that David claims that those sitting at the table with him are his enemies and not God's. But it simply can't be true. Some scriptures plainly state that God has enemies. Right? The apostle Paul declared, "For if, while we were God's enemies, we were reconciled to him through the death of his Son, how much more, having been reconciled, shall we be saved through his life!" (Romans 5:10, NIV) How can I honestly question whether God has enemies when Paul wrote that we were God's enemies?

WE SIMPLY CANNOT MAKE GOD BECOME OUR ENEMY.

Have you noticed how David sings that he's anointed at the table in the presence of his enemies, not God's enemies? Jesus teaches us to love our enemies, not His enemies. These are not small semantic distinctions. Just because we perceive people as being our enemies doesn't make them His enemies. Did you also notice that in the book of Romans, Paul throws us all together in the same group as God's enemies? We need some additional clarity! Let's add another perspective from Paul that will help us greatly. He declares:

> *Once you were alienated from God and were enemies in your minds because of your evil behavior. But now he has reconciled you by Christ's physical body through death to present you holy in his sight, without blemish and free from accusation.* —Colossians 1:21-22 (NIV)

I believe this is the truth that redeems our language of enemies. We thought we were enemies of God, but that belief was never reality.

The truth is that we all first approach God as enemies, not on His part, but on ours. This reality is hard to grasp because the lens of our experiences suggests that God postures Himself as an enemy, though He never will. He will certainly chase us down with a storm of divine intervention, similar to the pursuit of His beloved prophet-son Jonah. Yes, there are times when the love of God might bruise, but it's out of His desperate love to spare us destruction, similar to a parent tackling their child out of the way of oncoming traffic. We too often allow the consequences of our behavior to fuel the delusion that God is angry with us or out to harm us, but this simply is not true. We simply cannot make God become our enemy.

WAS SAUL (PAUL) AN ENEMY OF GOD?

When we first meet Saul in the Bible, I think we can all agree that he qualifies as an enemy of God. His introduction in the Scriptures goes like this:

> But Saul, still breathing threats and murder against the disciples of the Lord, went to the high priest and asked him for letters to the synagogues at Damascus, so that if he found any belonging to the Way, men or women, he might bring them bound to Jerusalem. —Acts 9:1-2

His focus is filled with threats and the desire to murder the disciples and any followers of the Way of Jesus. The ministry of death had so radicalized Saul (see 2 Corinthians 3:7) that he had become a hitman of sorts, representing the high priest of the temple, Caiaphas.

As Saul is on the road to Damascus, we read about an astonishing encounter:

> *Suddenly a light from heaven shone around him. And falling to the ground, he heard a voice saying to him, "Saul, Saul, why are you persecuting me?" And he said, "Who are you, Lord?" And he said, "I am Jesus, whom you are persecuting."* —Acts 9:3-5

There's much to unpack from this moment. The Lord doesn't hit Saul over the head or threaten to stone him; instead, He employs the "weapons of our warfare" that Paul would later write about. Jesus radically changed everything Saul thought he knew. This change of thought would transform Saul to such a degree that he would become one of the foremost apostolic voices in history. Saul first approached God as an enemy.

Did you notice the revelation that completely stopped Saul in his tracks? Jesus didn't plead his case to Saul or beg for mercy. Instead, Jesus spoke from the deep truths of mystical union and communicated that there was no difference between the people Saul was persecuting and Jesus Himself. Saul had never considered that he was not just persecuting people who followed Jesus but that he was literally persecuting Jesus. This truth so shifted the perspective of Saul that he ultimately went away to Arabia for more than three years to allow Holy Spirit to teach him the depths of this profound good news.

I humorously call this account in the book of Acts the Hollywood version of Saul's conversion. I can imagine the dramatic flashes of light, Saul falling to his knees, and the awe of those who were with him. But have you ever read what I call Paul's documentary version of this same account? In his own words, Paul declares:

> *For you have heard of my previous way of life in Judaism, how intensely I persecuted the church of God and tried*

to destroy it. I was advancing in Judaism beyond many of my own age among my people and was extremely zealous for the traditions of my fathers. But ... God, who set me apart from my mother's womb and called me by his grace, was pleased to reveal his Son in me. —Galatians 1:13-16 (NIV)

You can track the Galatians account right alongside the one we read in the books of Acts. There's Saul, persecuting the church, excelling in Judaism, and zealous for the traditions of his fathers. But look at the difference in the revelation Paul received in both accounts. In the book of Acts, Saul had a revelation that Jesus lived in people. In the book of Galatians, we discover that Paul had a revelation that Jesus also lived within him! This revelation would serve as the seedbed of what we now call "Union with Christ" which is affectionately known as Paul's gospel. Beautiful. How do we run this encounter through our salvation filters? Who led Saul to the Lord? When did he pray the sinner's prayer? He didn't go down the Romans Road; he hadn't written his letters to the church in Rome yet! Saul awakened to the revelation of the free gift of salvation. This is ultimately what God does to His enemies: He transforms them through forgiveness, love, and acceptance.

THIS IS ULTIMATELY WHAT GOD DOES TO HIS ENEMIES: HE TRANSFORMS THEM THROUGH FORGIVENESS, LOVE, AND ACCEPTANCE.

WAS JUDAS AN ENEMY OF GOD?

Maybe we can give Saul a pass. He, better known as Paul throughout history, would, after all, end up writing letters that would comprise the bulk of the New Testament. His revelation would serve as the foundation of our instruction concerning both the gospels of Union with Christ and Grace. Perhaps God was so gracious with him because He foresaw Paul's potential. But what about Judas? He must be an enemy of God! He betrayed Jesus, sold Him out, and his actions ultimately led to the crucifixion of our Lord. He eventually committed suicide, an act that many religious circles often deem as unforgivable. He is an enemy of God, no doubt. Or is he?

Let's go back and take a look at the pivotal moment when everyone knew that Judas must've been an enemy of Jesus. We all know the story well. Jesus is eating the Passover meal with His disciples, Judas included, and we witness something very troubling. Jesus says:

> *"Truly, I say to you, one of you will betray me." And they were very sorrowful and began to say to him, one after another, "Is it I, Lord?" He answered, "He who has dipped his hand in the dish with me will betray me. The Son of Man goes as it is written of him, but woe to that man by whom the Son of Man is betrayed! It would have been better for that man if he had not been born." Judas, who would betray him, answered, "Is it I, Rabbi?" He said to him, "You have said so." —Matthew 26:22-25*

Judas, remarkably, still feels free to dip with Jesus and partake of what would be the first communion.

I want to go on record and say that I do not believe Judas had nefarious intentions against Jesus. I don't believe that he thought his actions would lead to the crucifixion of Jesus. He could have possibly believed that he was speeding up what he thought would be the liberating actions of the Messiah against Rome. Judas's parents named him after Judah, the figurehead of the tribe from which it was prophesied the Messiah would emerge. Can you imagine the joy Judas felt when he knew that he was serving the Messiah, the Son of God, who was discipling him? There is no doubt in my heart: Judas loved Jesus deeply. But back to my first question about Judas: was he an enemy of God?

Let's reexamine a particular moment from the Last Supper one more time. According to the Seder (or Haggadah) tradition, which is the meal they were eating together at Passover, when you dipped bread into the sop or fish sauce, you didn't eat the bread yourself. Instead, you would give the bread you dipped to someone you loved. In keeping with this tradition, it makes perfect sense for Jesus to dip with Judas and hand him the bread to eat. In other words, Jesus knew exactly what Judas was about to do, but He loved him anyway. Here we see Judas posturing himself as an enemy of Jesus at the table, but Jesus simply would not withhold His love or communion from him. Judas approached Jesus as an enemy, but he discovered that he had a welcome place at the table.

Unfortunately, the delusion of Judas was too great, and his actions tormented him to the worst of ends. He ended up hanging himself on a tree at the edge of Gehenna, often mistranslated as hell (see Matthew 27:5). This seems like a fitting end to one of the worst men in history, but is this the end of the story? We are later informed in Acts 1:18 with another level of grotesque detail in the account of Judas's suicide, "Now this man acquired a field with the reward of his wickedness, and falling headlong he burst open in the middle and all his bowels gushed out." What is the point of adding this detail to the already miserable end of Judas? Why do we need to know that his bowels opened up during his self-inflicted hanging? Is this truth meant to solidify our rightful disdain for this enemy of God? Or is there yet more to the story of the one Jesus loved?

Can you picture Judas? Angry, tormented, and afraid. He betrayed the One who loved him most. The thought of living without such love became more than he could bear. He found a sturdy tree at the edge of hell (Gehenna) and did the unthinkable. Darkness was now inevitable, and justice, according to the law, had been served. His body began to empty out what remained inside. And that is where the story takes an unexpected plot twist. Do you remember what was in his belly? Did we forget that he still observed communion? Did we forget that he still ate the body of Jesus and drank His blood? From Judas poured bread and wine, communion, into Gehenna, and thusly prepared the arrival of Jesus into death, Sheol, and the grave.

THE TRUTH IS THAT WE ALL WERE ONCE JUDAS, BUT JESUS WOULD NEVER STOP LOVING US, EVEN THOUGH WE BETRAYED HIM. SUCH GOOD NEWS!

During the harrowing of hell (see 1 Peter 3:18-20), when Jesus descended into the grave, whose face do you believe He saw first? I submit that He first beheld Judas and embraced him, weeping tears of joy at their reunion. He then preached the gospel concerning Himself and led captivity captive. Jesus took the keys of death, Sheol, and the grave, and put a "closed for business" sign over the entrance. Judas was one of the first welcomed into the eternal kingdom of God. Jesus not only showed Judas that he had a place at His physical table despite his betrayal, but his seat remained perfectly intact at the eternal table of the Lord. The truth is that we all were once Judas, but Jesus would never stop loving us, even though we betrayed Him. Such good news!

LOVE YOUR ENEMIES

Although God's enemies—whether they are ours or those who present themselves as His—have chosen to hate, mistreat, or even kill God's Son or His children, God refuses to reciprocate as their enemy, and He calls us to follow His example. So, even when someone takes on the role of an enemy toward God or toward us, acting as a hostile opponent with the intent to harm, God responds with self-giving, radically forgiving love. The cross exemplifies this response, and it's this call to "love, pray for, and bless your enemies" that He asks us to embrace.

Perhaps this is how we reconcile Jesus's words, "Do not resist evil" (Matthew 5:39, author paraphrase), with Paul's exhortation, "Do not be overcome by evil, but overcome evil with good" (Romans 12:21, NIV). It's not that we do nothing in the face of evil. Instead, what Christ rejects is vengeance. Love and forgiveness overcome evil, even if that means martyrdom (as it has for so many). But doesn't that mean evil wins? Not if Easter morning has something to say about it. Evil does not win; death does not win—because they cannot get the final word. Love wins. Life wins. Light wins. Three beautiful names for Christ and Christ-in-us.

> **WHEN WE REALIZE THAT CHRIST ALONE IS OUR PEACE, WE ARE THEN TRULY ABLE TO WALK IN PEACE WITH ONE ANOTHER.**

So, while others may purposefully be enemies of God, God does not reciprocate their animosity. God is the enemy of no one. God is the Redeemer, Savior, and Deliverer of all. However, is there any non-human enemy toward which Christ has chosen to direct His hostility? To what enemy has the Lord become an enemy? In 1 Corinthians 15:26 (KJV), it is stated, "The last enemy that shall be destroyed is death." And Life Himself puts that enemy to death.

> *"The death of all was consummated in the Lord's body; yet, because the Word was in it, death and corruption were in the same act utterly abolished."*
> —Saint Athanasius[24]

When we realize that Christ alone is our peace, we are then truly able to walk in peace with one another. The late Dr. Martin Luther King Jr. shared the idea of the transformative power

---
24 Saint Athanasius, *On the Incarnation of the Word* (public domain).

of loving enemies when he said, "Now there is a final reason I think that Jesus says, 'Love your enemies.' It is this: that love has within it a redemptive power. And there is a power there that eventually transforms individuals."[25] All people who view themselves as enemies of God will one day come to an encounter with the One who is both their peace within and the source of their peace with everyone else. The work of the Lord concerning this issue will not end until humanity collectively declares that it no longer has enemies.

> "For he himself is our peace, who has made us both one and has broken down in his flesh the dividing wall of hostility by abolishing the law of commandments expressed in ordinances, that he might create in himself one new man in place of the two, so making peace, and might reconcile us both to God in one body through the cross, thereby killing the hostility."—Ephesians 2:14-16

---

25 King, Martin Luther, Jr. "Loving Your Enemies." Sermon at Dexter Avenue Baptist Church, Montgomery, Alabama, November 17, 1957.

CHAPTER 10

THE FATHER IS LIFE, LIGHT, AND LOVE

> *"For the glory of God is the living man, and the life of man is the vision of God. If the revelation of God by the creation already gives life to all the beings living on earth, how much more does the manifestation of the Father by the Word give life to those who see God!"*
> —Saint Irenaeus

It's once again fitting for us to visit the writings of John to discover the unchanging beauty and wonder of the character and nature of God. I believe that it was John's revelation of other-centered, self-sacrificial *agape* that inspired him to write on a much more mystical plane of truth than many of the other New Testament writings. John leans into truths about God that we could consider absolutes. But these rock-solid truths don't come across dogmatically; rather, they emanate as pure life, light, and love from the very Person of Jesus. The "otherness" of God does not threaten us; instead, we are invited to taste and see that He is good (see Psalm 34:8).

> **JOHN'S FIRST LETTER OPENS WITH A DECLARATION OF JESUS'S KEY MESSAGE: GOD IS LIFE, LIGHT, AND LOVE, AND THERE IS NO DARKNESS IN HIM.**

John's first letter opens with a declaration of Jesus's key message: God is Life, Light, and Love, and there is no darkness in Him. These declarations provide the bold clarity needed to understand the mystical truths he goes on to write about our beloved and trustworthy Father. Above all things and through all things, the Godhead reveals itself through these characteristics. There is no darkness, no more shadowy imagery concerning God. It's also of great comfort to discover that Jesus didn't reveal these things as something new about God, but about what He has ALWAYS been—Life, Light, and Love.

GOD IS LIFE

> *"Life was made manifest, and we have seen it, and testify to it and proclaim to you the eternal life, which was with the Father and was made manifest to us—that which we have seen and heard we proclaim also to you, so that you too may have fellowship with us; and indeed our fellowship is with the Father and with his Son Jesus Christ."*—1 John 1:1-4

By nature, God is life. He possesses life in Himself through the divine dance that we call *perichoresis*. Simply being the relational source of all living things enables the Father, Son, and Holy Spirit to eternally enjoy and reproduce life. This triune activity constitutes God's life. God's invisible and immaterial life-giving nature led Him to fittingly create the ages. He, who is Life, gives life. Understanding that God is life assures you that He will give you life. It's His very nature. Doubts fade when you realize that God's unchanging essence is life. If He has promised eternal life; He cannot lie. He is who He is, and that's the greatest blessing we could hope for.

That's why, for instance, the Father sent the Son to give life through the Spirit. The triune God's essence—Life, Light, and Love—is extended to us, His creation, so that we may have abundant life. So when we encounter Christ, who is our life (see Colossians 3:4), we can declare, "For with you is the fountain of life" (Psalm 36:9). This fountain will satisfy us forever because, as Jesus says, "Everyone who drinks of this water will be thirsty again, but whoever drinks of the water that I will give him will never be thirsty again. The water that I will give him will become in him a spring of water welling up to eternal life" (John 4:13-14).

Now that we have a basis for God as both the Source of all life and the Procreator of all living things, we might ponder the question, "What if God died?" What would happen if the Creator and Sustainer of all things ceased to breathe? This question is fully answered when we lean back into Trinitarian doctrine and a more robust Christology. When Jesus died on the cross, the entire Godhead—Father, Son, and Holy Spirit—died together. What's more is that all of creation died with the Trinity. We can begin to ponder the revelation of this truth as we understand what the writer of Hebrews reveals: "He [Jesus] is the radiance of the glory of God and the exact imprint of his nature, and he upholds the universe by the word of his power" (Hebrews 1:3). When Jesus died, all the Godhead died with Him. When the Word died, all things which were upheld died with Him. When God dies, all things must die with Him.

The apostle Paul rightly includes us all in the crucifixion of the Godhead (see Romans 6:3-14)! Every person ever conceived, as well as the whole of creation, was included in Jesus's death, burial, resurrection, and ascension. When Jesus was lifted up, God "dragged" all human beings to Himself (see John 12:32), and Jesus is the Savior of all humankind (see 1 Timothy 4:10). Furthermore, every human being is in Christ, and Christ is in them, and Christ is in the Father (see John 14:20). When Christ, the Creator in whom the cosmos was made, died, we all died. When Christ rose, we rose (see 2 Corinthians 5). If we believe that no one could escape dying when God died, is it unreasonable to believe that no one could escape being made alive at His resurrection?

> *"Christ was made man that we might be made God."*
> *"For the Lord touched all parts of creation, and freed and undeceived them all from every deceit."*
> *"He [Jesus] became what we are that He might make us what He is."*
> *"For no part of Creation is left void of him: he has filled all things everywhere."*
> —Saint Athanasius[26]

---

26 Saint Athanasius, *On the Incarnation of the Word* (public domain).

GOD IS LIGHT

> "This, in essence, is the message we heard from Christ and are passing on to you: God is light, pure light; there's not a trace of darkness in Him" —1 John 1:5 (MSG)

The ministry of death (the law) desperately tried to communicate, through its greatest prophet John the Baptist, that the true light was being revealed. The apostle John writes:
> The true light, which gives light to everyone, was coming into the world. He was in the world, and the world was made through him, yet the world did not know him. He came to his own, and his own people did not receive him. —John 1:9-11

The law could not communicate light because its reflections of God were twisted and distorted. It's no wonder then that the people could not receive Jesus. He looked nothing like their projected images or twisted violent expectations. The God who looks like Jesus appeared completely opposite to what the law displayed.

> **THE LAW COULD NOT COMMUNICATE LIGHT BECAUSE ITS REFLECTIONS OF GOD WERE TWISTED AND DISTORTED.**

God has always been light. This should deeply resonate with our hearts when we consider all the shadowy imagery we have attributed to Him through our own projections. Not only is God light, but He is also the Father of lights, as declared in James 1:17

(NIV), "Every good and perfect gift is from above, coming down from the Father of the heavenly lights, who does not change like shifting shadows." There are three profound truths to unpack from this verse:
1) You are a good and perfect gift.
2) You are a light who looks just like your *Abba*.
3) Your beloved Father never changes.

The relationship we have with God as light reflects our participation within *perichoresis* (the divine dance). We can contemplate this truth when Jesus says of Himself, "I am the light of the world. Whoever follows me will not walk in darkness, but will have the light of life" (John 8:12). This is not only true of Jesus, but it is also true of us! Jesus declares this clearly in the Sermon on the Mount when He says:

"You are the light of the world. A city set on a hill cannot be hidden. Nor do people light a lamp and put it under a basket, but on a stand, and it gives light to all in the house. In the same way, let your light shine before others, so that they may see your good works and give glory to your Father who is in heaven." —Matthew 5:14-16

We are the light of the world because He is the light of the world. We are children of light. This is the truth of our being. That being said, there have been times when we have lived in perceived darkness. The apostle Paul connected the idea that we were once in darkness because we forgot that we are meant to live as imitators of God as His beloved children. Paul declares, "For at one time you were darkness, but now you are light in the Lord. Walk as children of light (for the fruit of light is found in all that is good and right and true)" (Ephesians 5:8-9). In this truth, Paul begins to share the nuances of light. Light from God is, in its essence, good, right, and true. When we think of the light of God, consider this: He must be brighter than all we've believed about Him through shadows, or He is not the God that the apostles Paul and John are talking about.

IT IS THROUGH THE HUMAN AND DIVINE FACE OF JESUS CHRIST, WHICH IS RADIANT LIKE THE SUN IN ITS FULL STRENGTH, THAT LIGHT WILL ULTIMATELY TRANSFORM EVERYTHING IN CREATION.

While we search for God in a myriad of different things, it is the light of God that shines in the countenance of Jesus that gives us any authentic revelation of the indwelling hope of glory. Paul communicates this truth when he declares, "For God, who said, 'Let light shine out of darkness,' has shone in our hearts to give the light of the knowledge of the glory of God in the face of Jesus Christ" (2 Corinthians 4:6). It is through the human and divine face of Jesus Christ, which is radiant like the sun in its full strength, that light will ultimately transform everything in creation. It's a consuming fire that reveals the true essence of all things, and it redeems beyond all original goodness, heals every involvement in evil, and elevates us to participate in the divine nature. Beholding and participating in the light of God isn't primarily about comprehending the Scriptures but rather understanding God Himself, the divine

Logos. Thus, in illumination, we participate in the Son's clear knowledge of the Father.

GOD IS LOVE

> "It's not just that God loves us, it's that we're created within the love of God."
> —William P. Young[27]

Over the last several years, I have read, meditated on, and quoted 1 John 4 more times than I can recall. It has become one of my primary focuses when preaching the good news. I would also like to think that it has become more than a message and that more and more people are experiencing the fruit of *agape* in and through my life. Honestly, I couldn't care less about how theologically impressive a person is or how vast their influence or financial prowess may be; I'm searching for those who love well. I'm not saying that loving well means that you have finally reached the pinnacle of how to love as God loves, but it means being honest in the journey and growing daily in the love of God that cannot be exhausted.

The love of God is clearly self-sacrificial. The apostle John had a deep conviction of this facet of God's love, which is evident when he quotes Jesus as saying, "This is my commandment, that you love one another as I have loved you. Greater love has no one than this, that someone lay down his life for his friends" (John 15:12-13). The revelation of God's great love is simultaneously

---

[27] William Paul Young, "If Anything Matters Then Everything Matters," *Wm Paul Young*, https://wmpaulyoung.com/if-anything-matters-then-everything-matters/.

small enough to individually touch every human heart and grand enough to save the entire world (see John 3:16). In Greek, "world" is *kosmos*, which means universe. God's love is so vast that He saves all things procreated through His love, which encompasses everything that has been made.

The self-sacrificial love of God is also gloriously pervasive. It chases us into the depths of Sheol (the grave, hell) and remains tangible in the deepest darkness. David sings about this love:

> *If I ascend to heaven, you are there; If I make my bed in Sheol, behold, You are there. . . . Even darkness is not dark to You, And the night is as bright as the day. Darkness and light are alike to You"* —Psalm 139:8, 12 (NASB)

The apostle Paul picks up on this theme from David's cry and writes that there is absolutely nothing that can separate us from the love of God:

> *For I am sure that neither death nor life, nor angels nor rulers, nor things present nor things to come, nor powers, nor height nor depth, nor anything else in all creation, will be able to separate us from the love of God in Christ Jesus our Lord.* —Romans 8:38-39

AWAKENING TO GOD'S LOVE IS POSSIBLE ONLY BECAUSE WE HAVE FIRST BEEN EXPOSED TO SUCH GREAT LOVE.

The Western gospel's focus on sin and the delusion of distance and separation limits God's love as an experience for only those who reciprocate it. While this train of thought makes logical sense, it ignores the essence of *agape*, which is one-way in its offering. This means that God's unconditional love is always extended in our direction whether we respond to it or not. Furthermore, it is God's love that creates within us the capacity to love in the first place, as echoed in 1 John 4:19, "We love because he first loved us." Awakening to God's love is possible only because we have first been exposed to such great love. God doesn't love us because we believe everything correctly or are a member of the "right" church. It's not based on gender or economic status. He loves us because we have always been worthy of love.

There is loving discipline within the love of God, but there is no punishment. Nothing can separate us from the love of God, so there is no place, whether the grave, darkness, or the threat of non-existence that can diminish the all-encompassing love of God. The apostle John declares, "There is no fear in love, but perfect love casts out fear. For fear has to do with punishment, and whoever fears has not been perfected in love" (1 John 4:18). If there's anything you believe about the present love of God or the future possibilities of His love that produce any kind of fear in you, it is right to reject those beliefs and ask the Holy Spirit to reveal to you fresh revelations of the love of God that remains. There is no fear in love. There is no punishment in love. You exist because of the loving relationship of the Trinity. This is the truth of your being.

> *"All are invited to the peaceable and constructive ends of love—that weighty love from which all were*

created, to which all are called, and by which all have—already!—passed from death to life."
— Kenneth Tanner [28]

I always enjoy sharing the story of my discussion of love with my friend, Brian. He is now with the Lord, but through the years, I enjoyed his friendship, despite his professing atheism. The day I met him, the Holy Spirit spoke to my heart and told me that my only assignment for him was to love him. And that's what I set out to do.

One day we were driving together, and he made a joke about how people would find it humorous that one of the best friends of an atheist was a pastor. I turned to him and said, "You believe in God." He looked at me with surprise! I continued, "Brian, do you love your wife?"

He answered, "Yes."

I asked, "Do you love your son?"

"Of course," he answered.

I responded, "If you have known what it feels like to be loved and to love others, then you've had encounters with God. Love isn't something God simply does; it's Who God is."

I could see the power of this truth causing him to pause and ponder what he had just heard. I believe his perspective about God and love radically shifted that day. Furthermore, I am convinced that on the day of his passing, my dear friend and brother, a once professing atheist, found himself wrapped up in the arms of the God he had encountered many times as *agape* throughout his life.

---

[28] Kenneth Tanner, "All are invited to the peaceable and constructive ends of love—that weighty love from which all were created, to which all are called, and by which all have—already!—passed from death to life" tweet, X, 26 April 2024, 8:47 a.m., https://twitter.com/kennethtanner/status/1783840321648083215.

JUSTICE THROUGH LIFE, LIGHT, AND LOVE

The heart God has for justice lies in His ability to restore people when they are broken or hurt. He uses their mistakes to liberate, transform, and heal them. While some passages in the Hebrew Scriptures may appear, at surface level, to equate God's justice with vengeance on sinners, a closer look reveals that discipline is always meant to restore us back to the reality of our loving union. God's justice is always about saving and healing. What may seem like punishment is actually for the sake of restoration, not vengeance. Therefore, justice for the people means participating in God's wholeness and spaciousness and entering into His freedom.

I AM NOT ADVOCATING THAT JUSTICE IS A FIGMENT OF OUR IMAGINATIONS, BUT I AM SAYING THAT JUSTICE OUTSIDE OF LOVE IS VENGEANCE.

The apostle Paul specifically addresses self-righteous and judgmental people when he declares, "God's kindness is meant to lead you to repentance" (Romans 2:4). This thought is completely opposite to what many of us were taught about God's behavior. We were taught that God is severe with self-righteous, judgmental sinners! He will use whatever means necessary to show His great displeasure, be it storms, famine, war, sickness, etc. While we may have thought that God worked in such ways previously, none of these things appear to be good, even by human standards. And since the goodness of God far surpasses how we define human goodness, we can conclude that God's goodness is a better catalyst for our repentance than our own twisted and distorted desires for punitive justice and vengeance.

I am not advocating that justice is a figment of our imaginations, but I am saying that justice outside of love is vengeance. It is quite remarkable and otherworldly for us to consider that the justice of God is always restorative. God seeks to restore the child whom the ravages of war have displaced and the soldier who killed her parents. God seeks to restore the beaten wife and the abusive husband. God seeks to restore Barabbas, even though the cost of his freedom was the crucifixion of Jesus Christ. Certainly, God does not approve of abuse, murder, or taking advantage of your neighbor in any case. Yet, He is still the God who loves, forgives, and never forsakes people who do such things. This is why forgiveness, non-violence, and other-centered self-sacrificial *agape* are scandalous components of the gospel.

There is still a great deal of "I don't know" around the nuances of God's restorative justice, especially in a society so saturated with a punitive justice lens. I will say that I am convinced, based on the character and nature of God as revealed through the person of Jesus, that God hates no one. I also do not believe that God is actively executing any fresh judgments that fall outside the authority of Jesus. After all, they are one and the same. Jesus said of Himself, "For the Father judges no one, but has given all judgment to the Son" (John 5:22). Well then, there you go. Jesus is the judge! But wait, Jesus speaks further into this issue just a few chapters later in the book of John when He says, "If anyone hears my words and does not keep them, I do not judge him; for I did not come to judge the world but to save the world" (John 12:47).

Now, you may be asking, "People can just do whatever they want, and God still loves them and wants to restore them?" Yes, that's what I'm saying. People can do whatever they want, and God will never stop loving them, nor will He leave them. But does that mean nothing bad happens, that there's no suffering, that there is no chaos and destruction? Of course not. Just take a look around. It also doesn't mean the people closest to you won't walk away from you, hate you, divorce you, and take half of your stuff. Most often, we become the agents of our own suffering. Jesus goes on to say in John 12:48, "The one who rejects me and does not receive my words has a judge; the word that I have spoken will judge him on the last day."

Most of us have felt the harsh, real consequences of our actions and then blamed God for the suffering that follows. We feel justified in blaming our trustworthy Father for such things due to an overall distorted lens of His character and nature and a severe misunderstanding of God's sovereignty. Jesus allows the system of our fallen and twisted images of justice to take advantage of Him in order to reclaim it. He also does not punitively judge us but has manifested to save us. His restorative judgment is always unto righteousness (see Psalm 94:15; John 7:24). We hear the word "judgment," and our default is a pronouncement of guilt, but the verdict of Jesus is that we are His beloved children. That's good news!

WRATH THROUGH LIFE, LIGHT, AND LOVE

N. T. Wright says of the first-century Jews and Christians:

They were not understanding themselves as living in a narrative which said, "All humans are sinful and will go to hell; maybe God will be gracious and let us go to heaven instead and dwell with Him."[29]

The view of first-century Jews and Christians is radically different from our modern Western view. They did not see themselves as living in a world in which humanity was doomed to burn in the flames of God's wrath unless God intervened. There are no scriptures in the Old Testament that would suggest that Jews believed they were suffering under the wrath of God and looked to a future day when their Messiah would finally relieve them of His anger against them. Could it be that we've completely misunderstood the wrath of God?

GOD DID NOT POUR OUT WRATH ON JESUS TO SAVE THE WORLD, BUT IT WAS WRATH FROM JESUS THAT SAVED THE WORLD.

I want to be clear that wrath is real, and to deny it would be to deny God's love. You read that correctly: the wrath of God is a facet of His intense, never-ending love. The two words we translate to get the word "wrath" are *orgē* and *thymos*, and these words simply speak of displeasure or powerful emotion. The root *orgē* is where we get the modern word "orgasm." Talk about powerful emotion! I love Jeff Turner's insight into the manifestation of wrath when he says, "The wrath of God against sin is His forgiveness of it."[30] The *orgē* side of God's wrath is His powerful

---

[29] N.T. Wright, *Justification: God's Plan & Paul's Vision* (Lisle, IL: IVP Academic, February 11, 2016), 59.
[30] Jeff Turner (@JeffTurnerSOA), "The wrath of God against sin is His forgiveness of it," Twitter, August 6, 2017, 10:03 am, https://x.com/JeffTurnerSOA/status/894197148727881728/photo/1.

emotion against something, not against someone. It was wrath, the powerful emotion of God to set humanity free from sin, that caused Jesus to become the sin of the world. God did not pour out wrath on Jesus to save the world, but it was wrath from Jesus that saved the world.

Now let's take a look at the *thymos* component of wrath. *Thymos* is typically understood as "spirited" or "indignation." For our purposes, we will say that the *thymos* component of wrath can be considered God's strong displeasure. Paul declares, "The wrath of God is being revealed from heaven against all the godlessness and wickedness of people, who suppress the truth by their wickedness" (Romans 1:18, NIV). Notice here that God's displeasure isn't poured out on people but rather on what the people were doing. This is an important distinction to make. When you take into account the restorative nature of God, it makes sense that He hates all things that cause His beloved creation to live in darkness, wickedness, and ignorance of who they truly are in Christ.

Since God is not a control freak and the essence of His love is always what moves Him, He reluctantly "gives us over" to the things we relentlessly desire that can cause our eventual calamity. Think of it like this: God gives us both wisdom and warnings to spare us the eventual consequences of our actions. Should we continue to pursue what Paul called sinful desire, shameful lusts, and a depraved mind (see Romans 1:24-31), God will simply allow us to do what we want to do. This is a practical way to understand the *thymos* component of wrath. As we suffer not from God's pouring out of wrath but from the consequences of our actions, He never leaves nor forsakes us but suffers with us on the journey. What amazing love and grace! Furthermore, God continues to provide endless opportunities for restoration so that we can gain wisdom from our mistakes and greater confidence in His affection for us.

To finish out this chapter, I wanted to share some thoughts distilled directly from Brian Zhand's article called "God is Love. God is Love." I must agree with Brian and many of the other voices quoted throughout this book who would agree: of all the "things" God is, love reigns supreme.[31]

God is not wrath. Though we may ascribe the consequences of God's consent to our self-destructive will as His wrath, the truth remains that God is not wrath; God is love.

God is not a bloodthirsty deity who requires ritual killing. Though this may have been the only way we could understand God four millennia ago on the lower flanks of the holy mountain, the truth remains that God is not bloodthirsty; God is love.

God is not violence. Despite religion's long history of projecting violence onto God through our own sacrilege, the truth remains that God is love.

HE IS FLAWLESS IN EVERY ASPECT: AN OVERFLOWING WELLSPRING OF GOODNESS.

God does not operate an eternal torture chamber. However, we understand the state of a postmortem soul incapable of love, the truth remains that God is not a sadistic torturer who inflicts eternal pain; God is love.

---

31 Brian Zhand, "God is Love. God is Love," *Brian Zhand*, 16 March 2017, https://brianzahnd.com/2017/03/god-love-god-love/.

God is not a killer. Though many have misread the book of Revelation to such an extent that they think God's final solution for sin is the "Final Solution," the truth remains that God is not a genocidal killer; God is love.

There's no God who differs from Jesus. In the Son of God, we witness every perfection of God shining brightly—love, power, wisdom, justice, and majesty—all distinct from our sinful expectations. In the Son of God, we don't perceive a proud God, unwilling to show kindness. Instead, we see one who extends saving grace even when we were still sinners. In Him, we witness a glory unlike our selfish and needy desires for attention. We encounter a God of boundless generosity. He is flawless in every aspect: an overflowing wellspring of goodness. In Jesus—and only in Him—we discover the unveiled face of God, free from our "Rorschach Imagery," as one who is breathtakingly beautiful and captivates our hearts.

EPILOGUE

THE ROAD TO EMMAUS

Have you ever felt like you could identify with the two men on the road to Emmaus? Imagine these two distressed and traumatized fellas, grieved at what they saw happen to Jesus—His beating, crucifixion, and death. Both their experiences through their natural senses and the violated expectations of their hearts traumatized them. How would anyone recover from such trauma and disappointment? Emmaus was renowned for its healing hot springs, so perhaps a spa day was just what they needed. Can you picture it now? Let's use our imaginations and walk with these devastated men on their way to find some kind of healing, even if temporary, after what they witnessed happen to Jesus.

While these two men were en route, they had an unexpected traveler join them. I'm sure you've heard this story many times over, so you know that the traveler is Jesus. We know this now, but they didn't know it then. Jesus begins to engage them in conversation and asks some simple questions to get to the heart of the matter. It didn't take long. Almost immediately, the men not only shared the events around the horrific violence of Jesus's crucifixion but also the personal trauma they now carried, as they explained, "But we had hoped that he was the one to redeem

Israel" (Luke 24:21). So, here is the truth of the situation: these men are devastated, they've lost hope, and their beliefs are now lying in rubble. Let's go get in the hot tub and soak away in our misery. Sound familiar?

> **EVERYTHING THESE TWO MEN HAD HOPED FOR WAS UPENDED. NOW WOULD BE THE TIME, IT SEEMS, FOR JESUS TO EMBRACE AND CONSOLE THEM.**

Everything these two men had hoped for was upended. Now would be the time, it seems, for Jesus to embrace and console them. All He would need to do was reveal that He was Jesus, and their hope would have been instantly restored. Instead, Jesus begins with what appears to be a mild rebuke when He responds to their desperation, "O foolish ones, and slow of heart to believe all that the prophets have spoken! Was it not necessary that the Christ should suffer these things and enter into his glory?" (Luke 24:25-26). At Jesus's words, these men were certainly stirred. Jesus then proceeded to open all the scriptures from Moses and all the prophets, revealing where He had been throughout history and who He had always been. Do you see? Jesus allowed them to see the Scriptures through the lens of Christ to show them what they had been missing the whole time!

Once the party of three reached Emmaus for a planned spa day, Jesus was ready to move on, but these men compelled Him to stay. They sat down to eat bread with the Bread of Life, and suddenly recognized Jesus! What I particularly love about this encounter is that once Jesus had vanished, the men began to discuss how they felt when Jesus opened the Scriptures to them. They asked, "Did not our hearts burn within us while he talked to us on the road, while he opened to us the Scriptures?" (Luke 24:32) It would've been awesome to have the teaching notes from this profound encounter! These men were ready to soak in hot waters and grapple with their grief, but it was the revelation of Jesus throughout the Scriptures that caused the hot springs to bubble up from within their hearts! May we all have an experience like these men when we discover Jesus afresh throughout the whole of Scripture.

> **JESUS LOVES US TOO MUCH TO ALLOW US TO BECOME CASUALTIES OF OUR OWN SELF-SALVATION PROJECTS.**

I believe many within the church are undergoing a fresh "Emmaus Road" experience. The schizophrenic narcissist Rorschach God they've been taught to love and fear in Western Christianity has traumatized them. The condescending demands and attacks of those who worship a god in their own image have hurt them. We can only endure so much before it's time to step away and find healing, somehow, somewhere. The only One who can truly heal us is Someone we thought we already knew. Jesus loves us too much to allow us to become casualties of our own self-salvation projects. Therefore, He gently leads us back to rediscover the altogether lovely and transformative power of who the Godhead has always been—other-centered, self-sacrificial agape. In such encounters, even the coldest of hearts will once again be set ablaze!

SO GOOD TO BE TRUE

I'm sure you're familiar with the phrase "too good to be true." I've heard this many times over the years as I have earnestly sought out a clearer picture of the God who looks like Jesus. Now, I challenge people to ponder whether what they are hearing is indeed "so good to be true." I've certainly had my fair share of disagreements and pushback from people who say that God simply can't be as good as you believe. They argue that there's no way you can read the Bible and not see what is clearly there. They often warn, "You're heading down a slippery slope." Honestly, I had been going down slippery slopes already for years, worshiping a god who looked just like me. I was given the right to dislike people, be condescending and unloving, be a jerk on Facebook, and weaponize the good news with my political preferences. Trust me, I have lived on slippery slopes.

If the new slope I'm on looks more like loving people, loving God, and welcoming everyone to the table, then consider me guilty as charged. I'm not insisting that you simply take my word for it and take a vertical leap into questioning nearly everything you've previously believed, but I would challenge you to at least taste the "so good to be true" Christlike God and find out for yourself just how good He has always been.

"God is like Jesus. God has always been like Jesus. There has never been a time when God was not like Jesus. We have not always known what God is like—But now we do."
—Brian Zhand[32]

I WOULD CHALLENGE YOU TO AT LEAST TASTE THE "SO GOOD TO BE TRUE" CHRISTLIKE GOD AND FIND OUT FOR YOURSELF JUST HOW GOOD HE HAS ALWAYS BEEN.

WHAT ABOUT EMILY?

Emily once again sat nervously in the psychologist's office, her hands fidgeting with the edge of her sweater. Dr. Patel placed a series of inkblot cards in front of her. "Alright, Emily, I want you to tell me what you see in these images."

As she looked at the first card, she saw a splotch of ink that seemed to resemble a butterfly. But instead of describing what she saw, she closed her eyes for a moment and whispered a prayer.

"Jesus, help me see what You want me to see," she silently prayed.

When she opened her eyes again, she saw something different. The inkblot transformed into a pair of open hands, reaching out in love and compassion. She smiled, feeling a sense of warmth and peace wash over her.

"I see hands, open and welcoming," Emily said with confidence.

---

32 Brian Zhand, "God Is Like Jesus," *Brian Zhand*, 11 August 2011, https://brianzahnd.com/2011/08/god-is-like-jesus-2/.

Dr. Patel nodded and made a note on his pad. He showed her the next card, and again, Emily closed her eyes briefly, seeking guidance from her faith.

As she opened her eyes, the inkblot turned into a swirling pattern of light. She couldn't help but think of the verse from the Bible, "In him was life, and that life was the light of all mankind." She felt a surge of joy as she realized what she was seeing.

"It's light," she said, her voice filled with excitement. "Bright and radiant, like the light of Christ."

Dr. Patel raised an eyebrow, intrigued by her response but said nothing and moved on to the next card.

This time, Emily didn't even hesitate. As she looked at the inkblot, she saw a shape that resembled a heart. But it wasn't just any heart—it was a heart overflowing with love, pulsating with warmth and affection.

"It's a heart," Emily said softly, her eyes shining with tears of joy. "A heart filled with love, like the love of Jesus."

Dr. Patel looked at Emily with a mixture of surprise and curiosity. He had administered countless Rorschach tests, but he had never seen someone interpret the images in such a unique and profound way.

As the test continued, Emily continued to see images that reminded her of Jesus—images of forgiveness, compassion, and hope. With each inkblot, she felt her understanding of God deepen and her faith grow stronger.

When the test was finally over, Dr. Patel looked at Emily with a newfound respect. "You have a remarkable way of seeing the world, Emily," he said. "Your faith has given you a perspective that is truly inspiring."

Emily smiled, feeling grateful for the opportunity to share her faith with others. As she left the psychologist's office that day, she felt lighter and more joyful than she had in a long time. She knew that no matter what challenges lay ahead, she would always see the world through the eyes of the God who looks like Jesus—filled with life, light, and love.

A Simple Prayer

Heavenly Father, give me the courage to never stop thinking of You as more loving, good, and kind than all of my best guesses and experiences have allowed thus far. Amen.

Watch The Kingdom Is For Everyone with Matthew Hester!

the KINGDOM IS FOR EVERYONE
with Matthew Hester

GAN
GRACE AWAKENING NETWORK

Tuesdays 1pm EST and On-Demand on Roku and gantv.com
Episodes air same day on Youtube

PRESENT TRUTH
ACADEMY

www.PresentTruthAcademy.org

We offer resources that reclaim the image of God as we observe through the character and nature of Jesus

www.ingramcontent.com/pod-product-compliance
Lightning Source LLC
Chambersburg PA
CBHW050904160426
43194CB00011B/2286